ANI
ERII
GO

PARS

SARMATIÆ

ALBANIA

COLCHIS

GETÆ

Mare
Caspium
et
Hircanium

resq. qui est Ister

PontusEuximus

IBE-
RIA

MEDIA

PART

THRACIA

BI-
THINIA

PAPHLA-
GONIA

CAPPA-
DOCIA

ARME-
NIA

Tigris flu

ASSY-
RIA

ASIA MINOR

MESOPO-
TAMIA

PAMPHILIA

CILICIA

Euphrates flu

LYDIA

SIRIA

BABI-
LONIA

Sinus Persic
pars

Creta

Rhodus

Cyprus

IVDÆA

NEVM

PARS
ARABIA

ÆGYPTVS

RENE Ammoniaca Reg.

MARMARICA

Sinus Arabici pars

VM NOMEN TERRIS FATALE R

ROME™

ROME ™

JONATHAN STAMP

FOREWORD BY BRUNO HELLER

DESIGNED BY

STEPHEN SCHMIDT / DUUPLEX

HBO®   MELCHER MEDIA

ROME: THE COMPLETE
FIRST AND SECOND SEASONS
ARE NOW AVAILABLE ON DVD.

Published by

 MELCHER
MEDIA

124 West 13th Street
New York, NY 10011
www.melcher.com

In association with

PUBLISHER: Charles Melcher

ASSOCIATE PUBLISHER: Bonnie Eldon

EDITOR IN CHIEF: Duncan Bock

PRODUCTION DIRECTOR: Kurt Andrews

PROJECT EDITORS: Lindsey Stanberry and David E. Brown

Designed by Stephen Schmidt / DUUPLEX
www.duuplex.com

DESIGN ASSISTANTS: Sofia Valko and Gui Zong

Distributed in the U.S. by DK Publishing. www.dk.com

Library of Congress Control Number: 2007929575

ISBN-13: 978-1-59591-042-4

Printed in China

10 09 08 07   10 9 8 7 6 5 4 3 2 1

CONTENTS

ᘓ FOREWORD ᘔ

By BRUNO HELLER, CO-CREATOR AND EXECUTIVE PRODUCER

WHEN HBO APPROACHED ME ABOUT WRITING THE SHOW THAT BECAME *ROME,* I IMMEDIATELY JUMPED AT THE OPPORTUNITY. THEN I GOT VERY SCARED. THE FALL OF THE ROMAN REPUBLIC IS A STORY THAT HAS BEEN TOLD BRILLIANTLY MANY TIMES BEFORE.

How in the world could I make the story new and alive and relevant? The genre, so successfully executed in *I, Claudius* and more recently in *Gladiator,* would need to be completely reinvented to make it work for a modern television audience.

We started with the notion of telling the story from the perspective of two foot soldiers, Lucius Vorenus and Titus Pullo, the only two rank-and-file soldiers mentioned by Caesar in his *Commentaries on the Gallic Wars.* I realized that their working-class, "street" perspective was the key. What if we made the show as if it were a contemporary urban drama? As if it were shot on the actual streets of Republican Rome? Not the white marble and red velvet Rome of old sword-and-sandal movies, but the colorful, chaotic, crowded, dirty city that it was: a world of great beauty and abject squalor. What if we showed Romans the way they really were—in all their shocking pagan glory—without judging them and without imposing modern morality on them? What if we tried to create a TV drama that a Roman citizen of the late Republic might watch and recognize and enjoy?

We tend to think that people never change, that human nature is immutable, that human emotions translate across time and culture. Love is love; despair is despair. In fact, in many ways, the ancient Romans could not have been more different from us. By modern standards, they were an immoral people. If Caesar were alive today and doing the things he did, he might be ranked up there with Pol Pot and Stalin as a heinous war criminal. Endless warfare, mass slavery, public displays of brutal sadism, and unbridled sexuality were the lifeblood of Roman culture. The Romans were a cruel, lustful, avaricious, and violent people. They are us, but before monotheism and Freud taught us to be ashamed of ourselves. Romans celebrated the dark vices of the soul that we are taught to repress from infancy. Being true to that culture would open up *Rome* to accusations of exploitation—of using sex and violence to titillate and shock. It would have been much easier to make these characters sympathetic by not showing them as they really were. It was precisely this challenge that appealed: to bring that world to life in all its beauty and brutality yet succeed in making it relatable.

When we began to look for a place to create the show, we traveled to London, the United States, Bulgaria, Romania, and Tunisia. But everywhere we went, we felt that some intangible sense of reality was missing. And then we arrived at the fabled Cinecittà Studios in Rome. There, where *Ben Hur, Antony and Cleopatra,* and all of Fellini's masterpieces were shot, the light and air of ancient Rome was still alive, unchanged. The modern Romans, whom we would use to people the slums of the *Subura* and the benches of the Senate, were still as they were two thousand years ago, their gestures and idioms unaltered. They still carry themselves with hauteur and dignity; they still have a keen sense of life as theater.

We had to shoot the show in Rome.

And so we set about the task of re-creating a vanished world. If the audience was really to feel like they were stepping back in time, we had to create a living, breathing world completely from scratch. Every dress, every teacup, every knife had to be manufactured. Every word, every gesture, every emotion had to be true to the period. It was a monumental task, and all of us involved in the making of *Rome* are very proud of the results.

When the show aired, many people suggested it was an oblique commentary on the current state of American politics. Actually, any deliberate analogies of that kind were studiously avoided. Certainly, the story of the slow death of a republic and the painful birth of an empire resonates strongly today, but it rang the exact same bells in Napoleonic France and Victorian Britain. It rings bells in China and Liberia and Uzbekistan. In a thousand years' time, it will still be meaningful and resonant. As long as men and women love and hate and struggle for power and betray each other and seek redemption, the story of Rome will continue to be told.

OPPOSITE: Caesar basks in the glory of his Triumph procession.

INTRODUCTION

BY JONATHAN STAMP
CO-PRODUCER AND HISTORICAL CONSULTANT

I was a documentary filmmaker working for BBC Television in London when I first heard of HBO's plans for a major drama set in ancient Rome. The BBC was a co-producer of the series and was given an advance view of the first three scripts. They were sent to me because I was a graduate in Greek and Roman history and most of the documentaries I made were about the ancient world. I was the in-house Rome "expert" and so they asked me what I thought.

I read them and was immediately struck by how lively and fresh they felt, and how well they subverted the clichés that normally surrounded screen depictions of ancient Rome. This Rome felt real. It felt like an actual world inhabited by actual people, not the usual "HollyRome," a tired and over-familiar stage of pillars and marble. To me, it also felt very close to the spirit of the city I had studied for so long: swaggering, histrionic, cruel, sexy, earthy, unapologetic, bathed in fire and blood.

It was very exciting. That was what I thought and what I said. And I longed to be further involved in the production myself. In the end my wish was fulfilled and I became *Rome*'s historical consultant.

In this position, I was often asked, "Is it all true? Did it really happen that way?" The simple answer is, "No." *Rome* is not one hundred percent historically accurate and it was never meant to be. It is, after all, a drama, not a documentary, a distinction I was very clear about from the beginning. It was inspired by—and stayed close to—the actual events of the late Roman Republic, but it fictionalized them, filled in some gaps, and made some imaginative new connections. That was a huge part of the show's appeal for me.

But I am tempted to answer "Yes" to the question. *Rome* was not intended to be one hundred percent historically *accurate*, but we did everything we could to make it one hundred percent *authentic*. We made every possible effort to bring to life a world that an ancient Roman would have recognized, in all its details: from hairstyles to religious rituals, from the chain mail worn by Roman legionnaires during battle to the food served at an aristocratic dinner party. Every single element was considered.

From that point of view, I think *Rome* can claim to be the truest depiction of the subject ever brought to the screen. It's a grand statement, but I believe the pages of this book provide ample justification.

Here is the story of the end of the Roman Republic. Here is the story of Rome: the story of the death of one man, Caesar, whose assassination made way for the rise of another, Octavian. It's the story of their family, and of the men who rivaled them for power.

But it's also a story of those who served under them: of the ordinary men and women who walked the streets of Rome.

Rome is a tale of one city, but a tale uniquely told, not just from the top down but also from the bottom up. And it is, arguably, the tale of the most important, certainly the most tumultuous, years in that city's extraordinary history.

OPPOSITE: The view up the *Via Sacra* or Sacred Way, after a fresh rainfall.

DRAMATIS PERSONAE

JULIUS CAESAR
PLAYED BY Ciarán Hinds

MARK ANTONY
PLAYED BY James Purefoy

ATIA OF THE JULII
PLAYED BY Polly Walker

SERVILIA OF THE JUNII
PLAYED BY Lindsay Duncan

OCTAVIA OF THE JULII
PLAYED BY Kerry Condon

GAIUS OCTAVIAN (YOUNGER)
PLAYED BY Max Pirkis

MARCUS JUNIUS BRUTUS
PLAYED BY Tobias Menzies

POMPEY MAGNUS
PLAYED BY Kenneth Cranham

CLEOPATRA
PLAYED BY Lyndsey Marshal

LUCIUS VORENUS
PLAYED BY Kevin McKidd

NIOBE
PLAYED BY Indira Varma

TITUS PULLO
PLAYED BY Ray Stevenson

VORENA THE ELDER
PLAYED BY Coral Amiga

LYDE
PLAYED BY Esther Hall

EIRENE
PLAYED BY Chiara Mastalli

PORCIUS CATO
PLAYED BY Karl Johnson

MARCUS TULLIUS CICERO
PLAYED BY David Bamber

GAIUS OCTAVIAN (OLDER)
PLAYED BY Simon Woods

CALPURNIA
PLAYED BY Haydn Gwynne

POSCA
PLAYED BY Nicholas Woodeson

EVANDER PULCHIO
PLAYED BY Enzo Cilenti

MARCUS AGRIPPA
PLAYED BY Allen Leech

SCIPIO
PLAYED BY Paul Jesson

CASSIUS
PLAYED BY Guy Henry

QUINTUS POMPEY
PLAYED BY Rick Warden

CAESARION
PLAYED BY Max Baldry

ELENI
PLAYED BY Suzanne Bertish

LIVIA DRUSILLA
PLAYED BY Alice Henley

ERASTES FULMEN
PLAYED BY Lorcan Cranitch

TIMON
PLAYED BY Lee Boardman

LEVI
PLAYED BY Nigel Lindsay

GAIA
PLAYED BY Zuleikha Robinson

MAECENAS
PLAYED BY Alex Wyndham

MASCIUS
PLAYED BY Michael Nardone

LEPIDUS
PLAYED BY Ronan Vibert

JOCASTA
PLAYED BY Camilla Rutherford

September, 52 b.c. After six years of hard fighting, the Romans and the Gauls have arrived at their final showdown. At the battle of Alesia, in what is now northeastern France, Caesar's legions win a decisive victory.

SEASON ONE

THE CONQUEST OF GAUL

Julius Caesar accepts the surrender of Vercingetorix. The capture of the young nobleman, the leader of the Gallic resistance to Rome, effectively ended the war. Gaul, the area we now know as Belgium and France, became a Roman province. During the eight years of the Gallic War, Caesar is said to have killed more than one million men, enslaved a further million, and plundered more than 800 towns. For Caesar, Vercingetorix's surrender is the moment of triumph. He is now richer, and more powerful, than any Roman in history.

First-Spear Centurion Lucius Vorenus is in the thick of battle. It is the discipline and courage of soldiers like Vorenus that give the Romans the edge, even when facing overwhelming odds. At Alesia the Romans defeated a combined army of Gallic tribes that outnumbered them five to one.

IN FAVOR OF THE REPUBLIC

IN ROME CAESAR'S ENEMIES ATTEMP
TO RIDICULE HIS SUCCESS.

At a meeting of the Senate, Marcus Porcius Cat
raises a laugh by referring to Caesar as "the darlin
of Venus." Caesar's family, the Julii, claime
descent from Venus, the Roman goddess of love;
was a touch of effeminacy that his rivals use
against him.

But for all the apparent levity, Cato is deadl
serious. He is the leader of a faction in the Senat
that means to stop Caesar's meteoric rise at an
cost. That faction, the *Optimates*, or "Best Men,"
ultraconservative and resistant to any change. Th
Optimates have monopolized power and wealt
in Rome for centuries and have no intention of giv
ing them up.

On the other side of the Senate House are th
Populares, the "People Party," who want th
Roman people to have more say. Although he ha
been absent in Gaul for eight years, Caesa
remains the Populares' hero and leader.

That alone is enough to earn Cato's rivalry—and
his hatred. But Cato is also an old-style, dyed-in
the-wool supporter of the Republic. He believe
Caesar is courting the love of the people for on
reason: to make himself a king, or "to buy himsel
a crown," as Cato puts it.

Caesar aims to destroy the Republic—that is
Cato's message to the Senate. It is why he wears a
black toga, in ironic mourning for the Republic's
imminent demise.

But Cato has a plan: to relieve Caesar of his military command in Gaul and recall him to Rome
Stripped of his governorship of Gaul, Caesar wil
lose his legal immunity. He can then be tried in th
courts for crimes he is alleged to have committed
in the past and, if found guilty, he can be bank-
rupted and exiled.

A Fool's Errand

For Caesar, things seem to have taken a turn for the worse when bandits steal his army's standard—a golden eagle, the symbol of his reign. Losing the standard is a deep dishonor. Vorenus and Legionnaire Titus Pullo, both veterans of Caesar's famed Thirteenth Legion, are sent to recover it.

Despite their differences—Vorenus is honorable and pragmatic, while Pullo is arrogant and rebellious—the two make a formidable pair. They swiftly recover the standard and rescue Caesar's young nephew, Octavian, who was kidnapped en route to Caesar's camp.

VORENUS RETURNS TO ROME AFTER EIGHT YEARS OF FIGHTING IN GAUL. He is shocked at what he finds at home: his wife, Niobe, with a newborn in her arms. "What child is that?" he demands. Lucius, the son of his daughter, now of childbearing age, is her answer—an answer that will have to do, for now.

Caesar appoints his trusted deputy, Mark Antony, a Tribune of the People, and dispatches him to Rome to negotiate a compromise with the Senate. With his new title, Antony commands the power of veto of senatorial decisions, and he intends to use it. When a motion is set forth to recall Caesar and make him stand trial, a chaotic brawl breaks out on the Senate floor. No one hears Antony's veto. He must return the next day to veto the motion. Fearing for his safety, he is accompanied through the streets by Vorenus and Pullo. But a clash breaks out between the rival factions, and Antony never even makes it into the Senate House. The motion stands: Caesar is declared an enemy of Rome.

CROSSING THE RUBICON

✦ ⫘ ✦

"THIS IS A DARK DAY, AND I STAND AT A FORK IN THE ROAD."

—CAESAR

It's January, three years after Alesia, and Julius Caesar is taking the biggest gamble of his life. Either he accepts the verdict of the Senate and gives up his command, or he fights to defend himself. There was never much doubt as to which option Caesar, a man who in his own words valued "prestige more highly than life itself," would choose.

"They would have condemned me regardless of all my victories," Caesar wrote, "me—Gaius Caesar—had I not appealed to my army for help." And so Caesar contemplates the unthinkable: leading his legions under arms into Italy, something expressly forbidden by law, with the intention of marching them to Rome and making his case by force. Once he crosses the border into Italy, there will be no turning back. Caesar will no longer be a conquering hero; he will be a traitor.

A river—more of a stream, actually—marks the border. It is so puny that today its very whereabouts are disputed. It is called the Rubicon.

"Crossing the Rubicon" has passed into the language, a synonym for a decision so momentous that everything stands to be changed by it. Caesar, we're told, spent a sleepless night before he crossed his Rubicon, debating the consequences. Then, with an appropriate gambler's metaphor, he simply said, "The dice have been thrown." He would bear responsibility for where they landed.

In reality he already knew the outcome: civil war for Italy, for Rome, and for the whole world that Rome now commanded.

STEALING FROM SATURN

Cato and the Optimates have fled Rome, terrified at Caesar's sudden advance. They intend to rally troops to fight a rearguard action. For that they need money, which they have "borrowed" from the Roman State Treasury, held in the vaults of the Temple of Saturn.

The Treasury gold is stolen in transit and taken north, right into the path of Caesar's scouting mission, led by Vorenus and Pullo. The two are suspicious of the group of men wearing soldier's sandals and leading a wagon, and a bloody battle ensues. Vorenus, unaware of the wagon's cargo, leads the party onto Rome to post Caesar's proclamation of peace. But Pullo returns for the pretty slave girl, Eirene, and discovers the Treasury gold as well.

The stolen gold plotline dramatizes a question that has always vexed historians. Historically, Pompey left all the gold held in the Treasury of the Temple of Saturn when he abandoned Rome. But it is inexplicable that he would have done this when, in doing so, he effectively handed over the gold to Caesar, his enemy. The storyline is a good example of how the writers of *Rome* found imaginative explanations for events that are not completely explained by the historical record.

AT A CROSSROADS

CATO IS NO FOOL. NOW THAT WAR HAS BROKEN OUT, HE NEEDS TO ENLIST A REAL SOLDIER TO HELP HIM FIGHT AGAINST CAESAR.

Who better than Gnaeus Pompey? Known as Magnus or "The Great," Pompey is one of the most distinguished generals that Rome has ever produced. His prodigious exploits as a young man earned him the nickname "The Teenage Butcher."

Pompey had conquered much of the eastern Mediterranean for Rome, in the process earning himself fame and immense wealth. If anyone is capable of outmaneuvering Caesar on the battlefield, it is surely Pompey.

Winning Pompey to the cause of the Optimates was no easy task. Pompey was an admirer of Caesar and a former political colleague. He had secured his alliance with Caesar by marrying Caesar's daughter, Julia—a happy union, by all accounts, until her untimely death in childbirth.

But with Julia's death the ties with Caesar had been cut. And Cato successfully moved to make Pompey his man instead. Except Caesar surprised them all. Caesar's decision to cross the Rubicon and the extraordinary swiftness of his advance into Italy, caught even Pompey the Great by surprise.

It was the decision of Pompey, Cato's new ally, to withdraw from Rome to the south. He reasoned that Rome was indefensible, that it would be better to take a stand once he had had a chance to regroup. Cato, Scipio, and several members of the Senate had all believed him and followed him.

Now, in his tent on the road to Capua, the second city of Italy, Pompey is wracked by doubt. Can he raise an army to stand against Caesar here, or must he look to fight another day, and in another place?

NIOBE IS PLAYING HOSTESS AT A PARTY thrown to bless the new business
Vorenus has begun on his return to civilian life. But she is hardly feeling festive.
Lyde, her sister, confronts her with a threat. She knows that the baby Lucius is
really Niobe's son by Lyde's husband, Evander. It's a secret that could cost Niobe
her life, unless Lyde can be persuaded to keep it.

ATIA: *You naughty woman, you never told me Caesar had such a passion for you…I saw the way he looked at you. Like the bull that tupped Europa. I can't blame him. Such beauty…*

Secrets simmer across town, as well. Atia, Caesar's ambitious niece, throws a welcome-home party for her conquering uncle. One guest in particular has caught Atia's attention. Perfectly poised and immaculately connected, Servilia is one of the most prominent female aristocrats in Rome—and rumored to be the secret lover of Caesar. Atia can hardly credit the gossip, but she won't let Servilia out of her sight.

PULLO ARRIVES AT VORENUS'S HOME IN HOPES OF CELEBRATING HIS GOOD FORTUNE WITH HIS FRIEND. Luckily, he is just in time to turn the tables on Quintus, Pompey's son, who is looking for the stolen Treasury gold and threatens the lives of Vorenus and his family. With Pullo's help, they easily capture him. Pullo presents a bound-and-gagged Quintus to Caesar, who leaves Atia's homecoming party to meet them at the stables at the back of Atia's house. Caesar is astonished that Pullo knows the whereabouts of the gold. Such a stroke of good fortune seems a sign of divine favor. Pullo leads Caesar's men to the Treasury gold that he has buried in the hills outside of Rome.

CAESAR: *Legionary Pullo…You are a thief. But a foolish, incompetent thief. But you have served us well in the past. So we will pretend your foolishness is a species of honesty, and let you go unpunished. In fact I think we shall reward you. I do not like to quarrel with Fortune, and clearly she has taken you for a pet.*

LUCK IS NOT ALL ON CAESAR'S SIDE. Atia is jealous of his affair with Servilia and decides to make the clandestine relationship public knowledge. She commissions explicit graffiti, a crude cartoon of Caesar and Servilia caught in the act, to be plastered on every wall in Rome. Caesar and his wife, Calpurnia, discover the graffiti while they travel with their retinue through the streets. Laughter seems to follow them. Calpurnia is humiliated and furious with Caesar. And his faithful servant, Posca, is concerned: Calpurnia's family is very influential. Divorce would be devastating to Caesar's career. Caesar knows he must end the affair.

At home, Niobe receives an unexpected and unwelcome visitor. Despite his promises to stay away, Evander forces himself into the apartment to see his son and to confront his lover. Niobe knows that Vorenus would be within his rights to kill them both, and their child, if he comes to know of her infidelity. She is terrified that they will be discovered. And with reason. Pullo walks in on them. Now he too is party to their secret.

ON THE SOUTHERN COAST OF ROME, A SLAVE BRINGS POMPEY THE NEWS HE LEAST WANTS TO HEAR. The truce he has attempted to make with Caesar has been refused. War is now inevitable, but Pompey has no army with which to wage it. "What now?" Pompey ponders. "What now?" He has no choice but to raise an army abroad and lure Caesar to fight him there. He sails for Greece.

Caesar's affair with Servilia has delayed him in Rome and he is slow to follow Pompey to the coast. Though his armies were famed for their swiftness, on this occasion even he is not swift enough. When Caesar arrives at the coast, Pompey is gone.

The Masculine Arts

"It's high time you learned the masculine arts," Atia tells Octavian. "How to fight and copulate and skin animals and so forth."

Atia has great plans for her son Octavian, and she is desperate for him to win Caesar's favor. As Octavian is bookish and shy, she engages Pullo to tutor him in the ways of manhood. But she could not have imagined how Pullo would set about his task.

Octavian's initiation into manhood begins in the Roman sewers, where Pullo has lured Evander to extract the truth about his relationship with Niobe. Pullo has shared his doubts about Niobe's fidelity with Octavian, who has counseled caution. "It seems to me," says Octavian with typical acuity, "that suspicion alone is not enough to speak. Facts are necessary. Without facts you must remain silent."

And so he and Pullo bring Evander to a dark corner of the Cloaca Maxima, Rome's great sewer, to establish the facts. Pullo, the teacher, is amazed at the boldness and sang-froid of his young apprentice. When Evander refuses to speak, it is Octavian who suggests torturing him. Pullo objects, saying that he has never actually tortured anyone. The army has specialists for that, he admits. So Octavian improvises. "Cut off his thumbs."

"Juno's cunt, but you're salty," Pullo replies. "And I was worried about bringing you."

Octavian has certainly passed his initiation. When Evander finally reveals that he is the father of baby Lucius, Pullo stabs him repeatedly, killing him.

"We have buried this evil now," declares Octavian. "You must never speak of it again."

THE INEVITABLE SHOWDOWN BETWEEN THE ARMIES
OF CAESAR AND POMPEY TOOK PLACE IN THE LATE
SUMMER OF 48 B.C. AT PHARSALUS IN GREECE.

Despite being outnumbered nearly three to one, and leading an
army weakened by hunger, Caesar comprehensively defeated
Pompey. This was largely owing to overconfidence on Pompey's
part. When Caesar's army overran his camp after the battle, they
found it already dressed with banners celebrating Pompey's victory. Another debilitating component was that Pompey's army
contained many foreign mercenaries who could not communi-
cate easily with one another in the height of battle.

Caesar took no pleasure in his victory, despite its crucial
importance for his cause. He is said to have ridden around the
battlefield when Pompey's army took flight shouting, "Spare
your fellow Romans."

WE MERELY QUARRELED

———— ❧ ————

POMPEY FINDS HIMSELF WITHOUT FRIENDS AFTER THE
DEFEAT AT PHARSALUS. CATO AND SCIPIO DECIDE TO FLEE
TO AFRICA AND RAISE THEIR OWN ARMY TO CONTINUE
THE FIGHT—WITHOUT THE FORMER CONSUL OF ROME.

Another of Pompey's notable defectors was Marcus Junius Brutus.
Caesar regarded Brutus as a son. Indeed, some claimed that Brutus
really was Caesar's son. Servilia was Brutus's mother, and it was said
that Caesar had fathered him during their long-running affair.

It is almost certain that this was not true. Caesar was only fifteen
years old when Brutus was born, and his affair with Servilia did not
begin for another ten years. But there was unquestionably a close
bond of affection between the two men.

Brutus, however, had been torn between that affection and his con-
science. He was an ardent believer in the Roman Republic; indeed, he
was a direct descendent of Lucius Junius Brutus, who is regarded as
the founder of the Republic. He naturally sided with Cato and
Pompey, distrusting Caesar's monarchical ambitions. And so he had
found himself fighting on Pompey's side at Pharsalus.

Caesar gave special orders that Brutus should be spared if he gave
himself up, and that no violence should be done to him even if he
resisted. In the end, Brutus took the first option. Caesar, greeting
Brutus at his camp, is more than glad that he did so.

At dinner that evening, Mark Antony is less certain about Brutus's
change of heart and Caesar's acceptance of it. Caesar might call it
mercy, but Antony thinks it's weakness.

Cicero, seated to the far left, is another high-level defector to Caesar's
cause. The former supporter of the Republic is clearly uncomfortable
among Caesar's soldiers.

CAESAR PURSUES POMPEY TO EGYPT, where his rival retreated after the defeat at Pharsalus. Pompey hopes Egypt's rulers, the Ptolemies, will offer sanctuary. But the boy king, Ptolemy XIII, under the counsel of his courtiers, knows Pompey's cause is hopeless. It is Caesar who must be courted now. Pompey is brutally murdered by a member of Ptolemy's staff upon his arrival on Egyptian shores.

Caesar is unaware of Pompey's demise when King Ptolemy XIII receives him at the palace. Caesar is greeted with a gift—Pompey's head. It is not a welcome surprise. The courtiers are appalled at their misjudgment. Offending the most powerful man in the world could hardly be more serious. But they have an even bigger problem. Her name is Cleopatra.

CAESAR: SHAME ON THE HOUSE OF PTOLEMY FOR SUCH BARBARITY!
HE WAS A CONSUL OF ROME. A CONSUL OF ROME TO DIE IN THIS
SORDID WAY? QUARTERED LIKE SOME LOW THIEF? SHAME!

A CAPTIVE QUEEN

At the time of Caesar's arrival in Egypt, Cleopatra contests the legitimacy of her younger brother's right to the throne. Ptolemy XIII has the support of the Egyptian court, which holds Cleopatra in captivity in the Egyptian desert, together with her faithful servant, Charmian. Caesar knows of the instability of the Egyptian throne and plans to install himself as a mediator. But first he must find Cleopatra. Ptolemy XIII's supporters want to kill her before Caesar can rescue her.

CAESAR DISPATCHES PULLO AND VORENUS TO FIND CLEOPATRA AND BRING HER TO ALEXANDRIA. The mission is successful, especially for Pullo—he and Cleopatra spend a passionate night in the desert after she discovers she is ovulating. Upon her arrival in Alexandria, Cleopatra immediately charms Caesar, and they quickly form a relationship that is both political and sexual. Under Caesar's orders, Ptolemy XIII is murdered, his two most powerful courtiers are beheaded, and Cleopatra is installed as the puppet queen. Caesar's powers grow as he becomes the master of Egypt.

Nine months later, just before leaving Egypt, Caesar and Cleopatra present the material evidence of their new alliance: a son, Ptolemy Caesar, nicknamed Caesarion, "Little Caesar." But perhaps the baby's nickname should be "Little Pullo"?

SECRETS AND LIES

CAESAR ABANDONED SERVILIA AFTER THE REVELATION OF THEIR
AFFAIR. HEARTBROKEN, SHE IS DETERMINED TO GET REVENGE—BOTH
ON CAESAR FOR ENDING THE AFFAIR, AND ON ATIA FOR REVEALING IT.

The first stage of her vendetta is to befriend Atia's naïve and impressionable
daughter Octavia, whom Servilia is convinced she can manipulate.

Their friendship soon becomes a love affair, in the course of which Servilia
attempts to discover secrets she can use to harm Caesar. Servilia is intrigued
when Octavia mentions a "terrible affliction" of Caesar's that was witnessed
by her brother Octavian. She begs Octavia to discover the nature of the affliction, by any means necessary. Octavia goes so far as to seduce her own
brother but discovers nothing of the affliction. When she asks Octavian to tell
her a secret he has told no one else, the story he shares with his sister is that
of Evander and Niobe and his part in Evander's death.

The story is of little use to Servilia. But in return she is prepared to share
secrets of her own with Octavia. The most devastating of these is the revelation that Atia was responsible for the death of Octavia's husband, Glabius. In
shock, Octavia confronts Atia, who denies the accusation furiously. "I swear
on the spirits of my ancestors...on the stone of Jupiter, I did not kill your
husband." But Atia's real fury is reserved for Servilia. Now, more than ever,
she is determined to destroy her.

IN ROME, EMBOLDENED BY CAESAR'S SUCCESSES ABROAD, Atia takes her revenge on Servilia. Servilia is hunted down near the Forum and attacked by Atia's henchmen; she is stripped naked, her hair shorn, and left for dead.

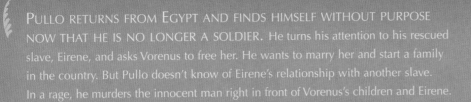

PULLO RETURNS FROM EGYPT AND FINDS HIMSELF WITHOUT PURPOSE
NOW THAT HE IS NO LONGER A SOLDIER. He turns his attention to his rescued
slave, Eirene, and asks Vorenus to free her. He wants to marry her and start a family
in the country. But Pullo doesn't know of Eirene's relationship with another slave.
In a rage, he murders the innocent man right in front of Vorenus's children and Eirene.

Vorenus's return to Rome is more successful. He is a hero and Caesar needs reliable men to run the city. Caesar persuades Vorenus, his most trusted lieutenant, to run for political office. Vorenus is no natural public speaker, but Niobe stands by his side, offering her support.

THE TRIUMPH

WITH THE DEFEAT OF CATO AND SCIPIO, CAESAR IS THE UNDISPUTED MASTER OF THE ROMAN WORLD.

The Senate votes unanimously to make him emperor of Rome. He celebrates his victories with a military Triumph.

On the appointed day, his face is ritually smeared with ox's blood. He wears the crown of Jupiter, fashioned of gold in the shape of an oak wreath. As the victorious general celebrating a Triumph, or *Triumphator* in Latin, he is momentarily considered to be as great as Jupiter, king of the Roman gods. For the day, Caesar is revered as if he were Jupiter himself.

During the procession, Caesar pauses at the Forum to ascend a podium, flanked by the members of his family and his most powerful supporters. The army that helped him secure his victory greets him, and the applause of the Roman crowd roars through the Forum.

Celebrating a Triumph was the most glorious day of any Roman's life and the peak of Caesar's ambitions. So intoxicating was the adulation that the *Triumphator* was assigned a special slave to travel in his chariot, to remind the general that even at this moment of ultimate achievement, he remained an ordinary man.

The words the slave recited in Latin were: *Respice post te, hominem te memento.* "Look behind you. Remember that you are only a mortal."

Words Caesar should not forget.

AFTER MURDERING VORENUS'S SLAVE, PULLO FINDS HIMSELF WITHOUT A HOME AND WITHOUT A PURPOSE.

A soldier with no more wars to wage, he has drifted into a life of crime. Found guilty of a murder, he is condemned to the gladiator arena and what seems a certain death.

Pullo has given up. He refuses to fight—until the gladiators begin to taunt him, ridiculing the one passion in Pullo's life: the Thirteenth Legion. Screaming "Thirteen!" Pullo takes down the men sent to kill him, one after another. The crowd goes wild. Then Pullo meets a one-eyed gladiator—a German who has never been defeated. The crowd grows hushed. It seems that an exhausted Pullo has fought his last battle.

Vorenus, watching from the sidelines, can take no more. Loyalty to Pullo, his comrade from the Thirteenth Legion and his closest friend, overrides his political responsibilities. Vorenus leaps into the arena and intervenes. Decisively.

VORENUS IS UNSURE THAT CAESAR WILL APPROVE OF HIS SAVING PULLO FROM THE GLADIATOR ARENA. Fearing exile—or worse—he takes his family to the countryside north of Rome, where Vorenus owns some farmland. He and Niobe joyfully inspect the land on which they hope to build a new farm and a new life. But their old life will not be so easily left behind.

CAESAR DOES NOT PUNISH VORENUS. He and Pullo are public heroes, and Caesar rewards Vorenus by appointing him a senator. "For the first few weeks, you'll stay close by me, learn the drill," Caesar tells him. He is accompanying Caesar through the Forum to the Senate, when Servilia's servant, Eleni, waylays him. Octavia had told Servilia Octavian's terrible secret. And in hearing the story of Evander, Servilia had also learned the name Vorenus. At the time it meant nothing, but now that Vorenus is renowned—and personally charged with the protection of Caesar's life—it is the weapon Servilia had sought for so long.

Eleni whispers the secret in Vorenus's ear. The boy Lucius, whom Vorenus believes to be his grandson, is in fact the son of his wife, Niobe, by another man. Vorenus wheels away in shock. In blind anger, he returns home to confront Niobe. Resigned to his rage, Niobe has a single request: that Vorenus should not harm Lucius. "The boy is blameless," she says and throws herself from the apartment balcony to her death.

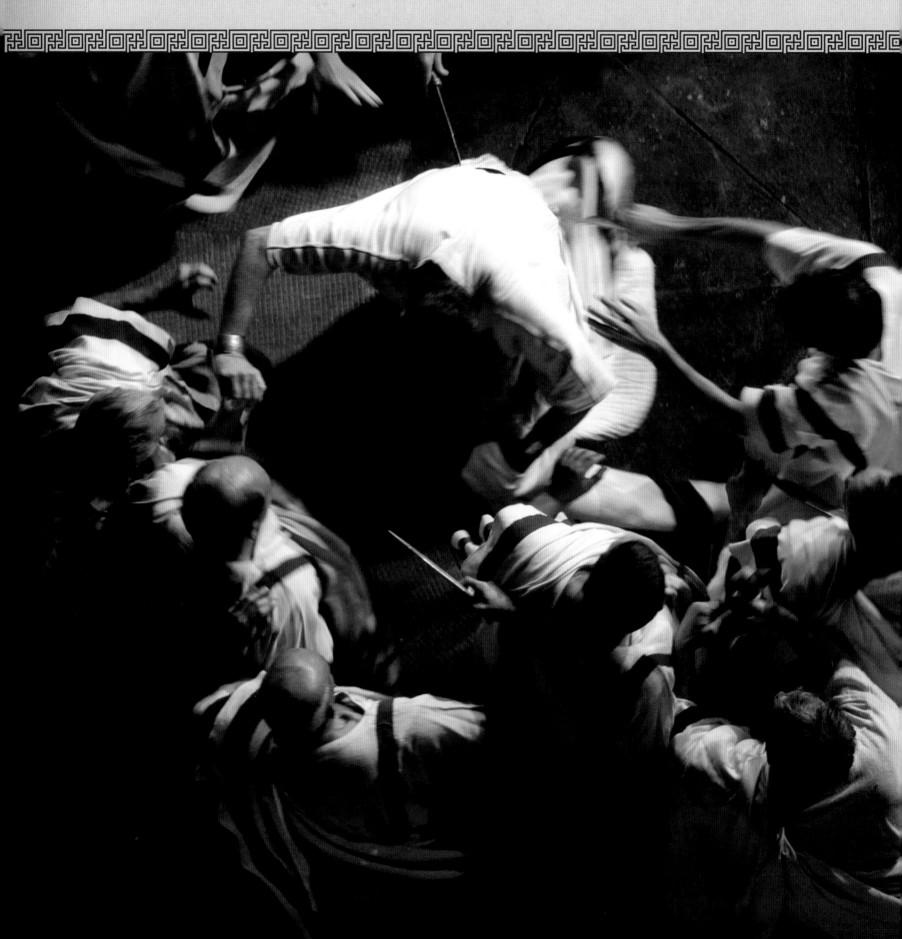

THE IDES OF MARCH

WITHOUT VORENUS, CAESAR ARRIVES AT THE SENATE HOUSE ALONE. NEVER HAS THE GREAT MAN BEEN MORE IN NEED OF PROTECTION.

Awaiting him is Brutus. At the urging of his vengeful mother, Servilia, and his envious co-conspirator, Cassius, Brutus is bracing himself to prove his manhood, restore the Republic—and murder his friend.

No sooner has Caesar entered the Senate House than Brutus, Cassius, and their fellow conspirators fall on him.

"Whichever way he turned he met the blows of daggers and saw the cold steel aimed at his face and at his eyes…and, like a wild beast trapped in a net, he had to suffer at the hands of each and every one of them: for they had agreed that they must all take part in the sacrifice and all flesh themselves with his blood."

So runs the description of the event by Greek writer Plutarch. It vividly captures the brutal reality of a moment that changed history, a moment that has become a myth: the assassination of Julius Caesar, the Ides of March.

Plutarch described how the conspirators gathered around Caesar as soon as he entered the Senate House and attacked on the prearranged signal: one of them would pull on Caesar's toga. What followed was panic. The first blow, delivered by a conspirator called Casca, hardly drew blood. Perhaps he was so overawed by the immensity of what he was about to do that he could scarcely hold his knife.

And then the others closed in, stabbing wildly and mostly to no great effect. In the process, according to Plutarch, "many of his assailants were wounded by each other, as they tried to plant all those blows in one body." Caesar appears to have said nothing throughout the attack. The famous "Et tu, Brute?" was Shakespeare's invention.

Caesar's life was taken amid a scrum of scrabbling, terrified men.

Struck by twenty-three blows, Caesar was mortally wounded by the second. This is known from his autopsy, the earliest recorded autopsy in history.

"Thus ever for tyrants!" declares Cassius.

TOGAS AND TUNICS
～ DRESSING ROME ～

"ONCE I STARTED TO DO MY OWN RESEARCH—IN BOOKS, IN MUSEUMS—IT DAWNED ON ME THAT SO MUCH OF WHAT YOU SEE IN FILMS OF THE PERIOD IS WRONG," SAYS APRIL FERRY, THE ACADEMY AWARD–NOMINATED COSTUME DESIGNER FOR *ROME*. "IN KEEPING WITH THE AMBITION OF THE WHOLE PRODUCTION, WE DIDN'T WANT TO REPEAT THOSE MISTAKES. WE WANTED TO GET IT RIGHT WHEREVER WE COULD. AUTHENTICITY WAS REALLY IMPORTANT TO US."

The task facing the costume designers and creators of *Rome* was an enormous one. The commitment to authenticity meant creating the entire wardrobe from scratch. This amounted to more than 4,000 items for the first season of the series, with 2,500 pieces required for the first three episodes alone.

Every stage of the process was carefully managed in order to preserve the genuine ancient Roman look and feel. Ferry worked exclusively with fabrics that would have been available during ancient Roman times. Cotton, wool, linen, and silk were all purchased in their natural state and then treated and hand-dyed on set. Much of the raw fabric came from India, which Ferry visited several times while working on the show. The rest came from Morocco, Tunisia, and Prato in northern Italy.

Working with the original fabric gave the clothes not only the right texture and color, but also the proper weight. "With items of clothing like the toga, which was basically fabric draped on the body, that was a very important detail to get right. The way the garment hangs is an essential part of the way that it looks," explains Ferry.

The costumers of *Rome* were not limited to creating the world of ancient Rome itself. In dressing Cleopatra and creating the Ptolemaic court at Alexandria, there was also the creation of an entirely different Egyptian look.

"It was a particular challenge to create a look for Cleopatra because she is such a familiar figure," says Ferry. "She's a myth, and it's hard to dress a myth. One of the most important things for me—and for hair and makeup, who designed her wonderful wigs—was just to shake it up a bit. I did my research and then I used my imagination. I was very much influenced by the particular shape of Lyndsey Marshall. You've got this tiny, beautifully shaped little woman, not voluptuous like we're told the real Cleopatra was, but very bold, very sexy, and prepared to take risks. If you look at what we asked her to wear, it's nearly always transparent, and she had nothing on underneath. At the very least, it's figure hugging. And it all makes her look so striking and sexy. It makes perfect sense why Caesar and Antony fell for her."

But even the task of re-creating Egypt was one Ferry found was best faced from her office in Rome. "One of the advantages of working in Rome is that the standard of craftsmanship is so extremely high," she says. In some cases the most efficient way to work was to create prototypes of certain objects in Rome and then have them replicated abroad. The leather breastplate worn by Roman army officers, such as Lucius Vorenus, was created at Cinecittà Studios in Rome and then replicated in India.

The process was repeated with much of the specially created jewelry worn by Roman matrons, as well as the helmets, buckles, belts, insignia, and chain mail worn by the Roman legionnaires. Each chain mail tunic weighed thirty-six pounds. From a prototype created in Rome, an additional 250 were made in India.

Designing the costumes for *Rome* was a huge undertaking, but Ferry found the process intensely rewarding. "This is perhaps the single most fulfilling assignment I've ever undertaken in nearly fifty years in the business," says Ferry.

THE TOGA

The desire to be true to the period of ancient Rome was a discipline for the show's costumers, but not necessarily a restriction. "The traditional 'white toga' look that tends to dominate Roman costume dramas is not simply boring, it's wrong," says costume designer, April Ferry. In reality there was tremendous variety in Roman dress. Even the toga, the traditional upper-class male garment, varied a lot. There was the pure white toga worn by those running for political office, but there were also striped togas, bordered togas, even a toga of solid purple, embroidered with gold, that was only worn by a general during the day of a military Triumph.

PLEBEIANS

Women's fashion denoted status in ancient Rome as clearly as it does today. Costume designer April Ferry took this into account when creating costumes for the plebeian women of *Rome*, including Eirene, Niobe, and Vorena the Elder.

The quality of their clothing is reflected in the small details, including the colors and fabrics used to create the dresses. Their dresses tended to be in shades of green, lilac, and blue. These dyes were less expensive and often associated with plebeian women. The dresses were designed in wool or linen rather than the rarefied and expensive silk used to make costumes for patrician matrons, such as Servilia or Atia.

Eirene, dressed up in the Treasury gold, and Niobe, in her finest for the party she and Vorenus throw for his new business, show the plebeian woman's penchant for elaborate and gaudy jewelry. Patrician women tended to prefer less ostentatious rings and broaches.

"STEALIN JUPITER"

NIOBE dressed for the party

⚜ WARRIORS ⚜

April Ferry carefully re-created the military style of late Republican Rome. Much attention was paid to every detail of a soldier's costume, from the chain mail to the sandals.

The legionnaires, including Vorenus and Pullo, wore a cuirass, a protective breastplate molded from wet leather. The cuirass is of ancient Greek origin. The *phalera*, or disc, at the center of the cuirass is a military decoration awarded for valor.

Pullo's footwear, the *caliga*, was standard issue for a Roman legionnaire. It was made of leather and reinforced with hobnails. The hobnails made the sandals last longer, but they also made the shoe a weapon of sorts. A swift kick with a *caliga* could inflict real pain.

Vorenus and Mark Antony are wearing Montefortino helmets, the classic Roman military helmet. It was normally made of iron or copper alloy. The helmet had a lip protruding at the back to protect the neck, a brow guard, and two cheek pieces. The color of the plumage on the crest denoted the rank of the wearer.

ROME

"HOW TITUS P. etc"

MARK ANTONY

PATRICIAN WOMEN

The process of preparing the mistress of the house began shortly after dawn, under the supervision of a slave known as an *ornatrix*. The *ornatrix* also had the important responsibility of styling her mistress's hair.

Patrician women vied with each other to have the most elaborate hairstyles, even though they covered their heads in public. Typical styles featured masses of curls, sometimes piled high on a wire framework. These elaborate hairstyles required much time and attention.

Roman women liked to dye their hair. Black and reddish-brown were popular colors. They also wore wigs. Slaves provided hair for the wigs: fair hair from the Baltic and Germany and black hair from India were highly prized.

Cosmetics were mainly made from crushed minerals, such as chalk and plant extracts, such as saffron. A body slave would apply the makeup. Mirrors were made of burnished metal.

Atia admits to the importance of a good body slave when she eyes Servilia enviously at her welcome-home party for Caesar: "She has a good cosmetics slave, I'll grant you," she whispers slyly to her servant Merula. "But a lover for Caesar? Absurd."

ROME

ATIA

FAR FROM THE CITY, UNAWARE OF THE TROUBLE UNFOLDING,
PULLO HAS A REQUEST OF EIRENE. "I know I didn't get us started on
the right foot, killing your man and all," he begins, "but...with permission
of Mars and Venus, I ask you to be my wife." Roman marriage required
no set form of words, nor a written contract, but simply mutual consent.
Pullo asks; Eirene says yes. And there in the glade they are wed.

We Shall Mourn the Man and Burn the Tyrant

Funerals were the most impressive of all Roman state occasions. As part of the procession, the dead man's retinue carried masks of his ancestors.

Arrangements for Caesar's funeral are shared between Brutus and Cassius, the men responsible for his death, and Mark Antony, the man determined to avenge it. They face each other across Caesar's body in an uneasy truce.

A truce that would not last.

Rome is reeling after the death of Caesar. To universal amazement, Caesar's will named eighteen-year-old Octavian as his sole heir.

Despite Antony and Atia's desire to leave the city, Octavian insists they stay, so he can defend his rights and status as Caesar's son. And he has discovered a legal loophole that may put Caesar's murderers at a disadvantage. It is this loophole that leads to a public funeral for Caesar, where both Brutus and Antony speak.

Plutarch recorded a historical account of Antony's funeral oration, and Shakespeare immortalized it in his play *Julius Caesar*. The powerful words turned the grieving Roman mob against the men who killed Caesar.

Brutus and Cassius have gambled and lost. They may have prominent supporters, but Antony has the upper hand. "I have an angry mob that will roast and eat your men of quality in the ashes of the Senate House," he threatens.

Brutus and Cassius are forced to flee Rome. Less than a week after cheating death, Antony is the new master of the empire.

EXACTING REVENGE

Antony managed to escape death after Caesar's assassination, but it follows Vorenus doggedly. He was tricked into abandoning Caesar. He watched his wife commit suicide. And finally he learned that his children and his sister-in-law, Lyde, were brutally murdered by local crimelord Erastes Fulmen.

Vorenus earned the wrath of Erastes when he interfered with his henchmen harassing a local merchant. Vorenus failed to make a public apology in the Forum, so Erastes took his terrible revenge. Vorenus, wandering the streets, inconsolable after the death of his wife, was not there to protect his children and Lyde.

With the help of Pullo, Vorenus avenges their deaths. Grief-stricken, he takes a memento with him: Erastes's head.

CLEOPATRA, IN ROME TO MOURN THE DEATH OF CAESAR, has a proposal for Mark Antony: if he were to publicly recognize her son, Caesarion, as Caesar's lawful son, then she would show Antony her "eternal gratitude." He scoffs at the idea. Atia hosts a dinner party in Cleopatra's honor, but she cannot conceal her jealousy for the beautiful young queen who openly flirts with Antony. "Die screaming, you pigspawn trollop," Atia whispers in her ear on parting.

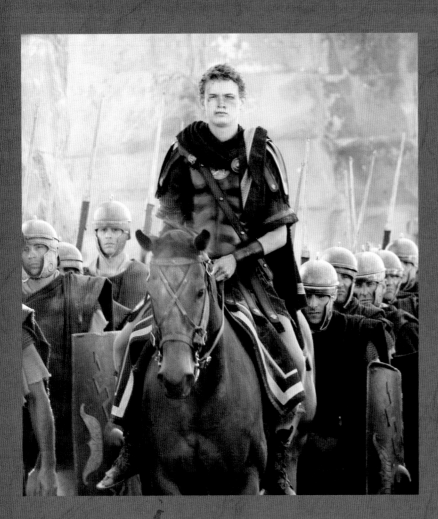

Still bruised from a vicious beating at the hands of Mark Antony, Octavian leaves Rome. He is headed south for an important meeting. The Senate has decided to exploit the rift between Antony and Octavian. And so, Octavian meets with Cicero in the south, where he agrees to an alliance against Antony. Everyone around him sees Octavian as a boy whom they can manipulate. But Octavian is already looking to a future in which he will manipulate them.

THE SON OF HADES

WITH ERASTES FULMEN DEAD, VORENUS ASSUMES THE ROLE OF CAPTAIN OF THE AVENTINE COLLEGIUM.

He wastes no time establishing his reputation: at a peaceful meeting of rival gangs, he smashes the statue of the goddess Concordia and declares himself a son of Hades. The gang leaders are shocked.

Vorenus welcomes both his enemies' fear and respect. But Pullo worries that Vorenus has also earned their hatred, not to mention the wrath of the gods. "You're no son of Hades," Pullo growls. "The gods do not like that sort of shit from mortal men."

Some men are impressed by the rumors of the "black-hearted villain" who is now running the Aventine. One of these men, Mascius, a former soldier for the Thirteenth Legion, comes to the Aventine looking for a job. Homeless after losing his farm, he joins them, despite the questionable nature of the work.

The Aventine Collegium controlled the docks on the river Tiber, and the docks controlled the grain shipments from Egypt, without which the city would starve. Originally, collegia were trade unions, but in late Republican Rome they had undergone a change. Many were no longer much more than fronts for organized crime. Their captains were powerful, dangerous men— mob bosses, effectively—often with influential political connections. The Aventine was perhaps the most powerful of all the city's collegia, and it made the captain of the Aventine a very powerful man.

THESE BEING THE WORDS OF
MARCUS TULLIUS CICERO

Mark Antony comes to the Senate House expecting Cicero to offer him a prize post, the governorship of Gaul, when his term as consul expires. What he hears is very different. Cicero, who has left Rome for the south, has prepared a speech to be read by the clerk in his absence.

"Please listen as if you were sober and intelligent, and not a drink-sodden, sex-addled wreck. ...You have brought upon us war, pestilence, and destruction. You are Rome's Helen of Troy. But then...a woman's role has always suited you best."

In a rage, Antony begins to bludgeon the clerk with all his might. He looks up to find the Senate deserted.

The war between Antony and the Senate has begun.

The historical record shows that Antony did not actually bludgeon the clerk to death when Cicero's famously insulting diatribe was read in the Senate, but the rest of this plotline, including Antony's attempt to secure governorship of Gaul, is absolutely true.

Cicero made a series of devastating attacks on Antony in 44 and 43 B.C. These speeches are known as the *Philippics*, after a series of speeches by the Greek orator Demosthenes that attacked Philip of Macedon, father of Alexander the Great.

The *Philippics* contain some of the most brilliant invective Cicero ever wrote. Some of the lines in the script, including the quip about a woman's role suiting Antony best, are direct quotations.

WITH BRUTUS AND CASSIUS GONE, SERVILIA IS VIRTUALLY DEFENSELESS.
She makes a desperate attempt to poison her rival Atia, which fails. Atia's men kidnap
Servilia to take a terrible revenge. She is alone and at their mercy. When Atia becomes
exasperated with Servilia's resilience, she insists her henchman Timon "cut off her
face." But he is pushed too far. He cuts Servilia free and helps her escape.

Octavian is victorious over Mark Antony. As he marches to Rome with his troops, he meets Pullo, who is desperately searching for Vorenus among the dead. Pullo has learned that Vorenus's children are alive and he wants to tell his friend the good news. Octavian is quick to offer his help in the search for Vorenus. He provides Pullo the protection of his seal, along with a swift horse. Pullo gladly accepts.

OCTAVIAN: I SPEAK TO YOU NOW
NOT AS A SOLDIER OR CITIZEN, BUT
AS A GRIEVING SON…AS MY FIRST
ACT IN THIS REBORN REPUBLIC,
AND IN HONOR OF MY FATHER,
I PROPOSE A MOTION TO DECLARE
BRUTUS AND CASSIUS MURDERERS
AND ENEMIES OF THE STATE.

Octavian returns to Rome victorious, but the Senate believes that it can still dominate him and they refuse him the honor of a Triumph. Cicero reluctantly agrees to give Octavian the title of consul, on the condition that the boy except his guidance. "I am well aware of my inexperience. I will not utter a word without your advice," Octavian promises.

On the day of his swearing in, Octavian takes the floor and speaks without Cicero's approval. The senators listen in terrified silence as Octavian motions to declare Brutus and Cassius the murderers of Caesar and enemies of the State. Cicero is horrified; Octavian has effectively severed his relationship with the Senate.

Circero joins forces with Brutus and Cassius, who have quietly been building an army. Octavian finds himself without powerful friends.

WHEN ATIA LEARNS THAT THE SENATE HAS TURNED ON HER SON, SHE DEVISES A PLAN TO UNITE OCTAVIAN AND MARK ANTONY. She arrives at Antony's camp, far north of Rome, draped in furs and riding a white horse. She is an apparition of beauty amid the dirty soldiers. Atia and Antony waste no time getting reacquainted. Only afterward does Antony wonder how she arrived at his camp unaccompanied. But Atia is not alone.

AN ALLIANCE IS FORMED

OCTAVIAN TRAVELED NORTH WITH HIS MOTHER TO MARK ANTONY'S CAMP IN HOPES OF FORMING AN ALLIANCE WITH HIS RIVAL.

United, they completely, and unexpectedly, shifted the balance of power. The Senate lost its upper hand and would never recover its former influence.

A third man, Marcus Aemilius Lepidus, was included in the alliance, which became known as the Triumvirate, or the "Rule of Three Men." Lepidus was of noble family but lacked the drive and ambition normally associated with a Roman of his class. He accepted his inferior status in the Triumvirate for some years before making an ill-judged military move against Octavian. This gave Octavian the excuse he needed to sideline Lepidus completely. He ended his life under ignominious house arrest.

The Triumvirs appointed themselves to power for five years. Their authority was virtually absolute. They divided the Roman world into three spheres of influence, one sphere for each of them. They also resolved not to repeat a mistake that they believed had ruined Caesar. Where he had shown clemency to his enemies, they would exact vengeance from them. History had proved that mercy did not pay.

Those who knew Antony or Octavian recognized that the alliance could only be temporary. Both were too ambitious to accept the sharing of power for long. They would continue to maneuver for position within the alliance, each believing that he had the measure of the other, until the moment of the final showdown came.

But that was for the future.

IT'S A TIME OF RENEWED ALLIANCES. While Octavian and Antony join forces against the Senate, Pullo and Vorenus are reunited for a simpler task. Together, they rescue Vorenus's children from the slave camp in which they've been held and return with them to Rome. Vorenus has dreams of a new, happier life with them there and hopes to reconcile past mistakes. Maybe once again they can be a family.

Octavian decides that he and Mark Antony must kill Brutus and Cassius's most ardent supporters before their alliance is revealed. Lepidus is shocked to find some of the finest men in Rome on the list. Octavian gives the list to Vorenus, who divides the names among the gangs of the Aventine. At the top of the list is Cicero. Pullo is sent to do the deed.

At Philippi in Greece, Octavian and Mark Antony's united forces easily defeat the army raised by Cassius and Brutus. Cassius is mortally wounded. Knowing that death is imminent, Brutus asks the aide-de-camp to send word to his mother and then draws his sword and runs into the swarm of oncoming soldiers.

BRUTUS: *Give my best to my mother. Tell her something…*
Tell her something suitable.

THERE IS TENSION BETWEEN THE WOMEN OF THE AVENTINE. GAIA, THE NEWLY HIRED HAND, has every man in the collegium wrapped around her finger, and as Pullo's wife, Eirene, knows all too well, that includes Pullo. When Eirene insists that Pullo punish Gaia for her disrespect, Pullo agrees, but in the end it's not a beating that he administers to her. It's the beginning of a love triangle that will end in tragedy for all three. And from which two will not emerge alive.

"I know you very well. You are kind and full-hearted and beautiful and I would tear down the sky if you asked me to." It's more than just adoration, it's love, and Octavia has been craving it. But the man who is opening his heart to her is one Marcus Vipsanius Agrippa, who is Octavian's closest friend and trusted advisor. This is a love affair Octavian will not approve of and both Agrippa and Octavia know it.

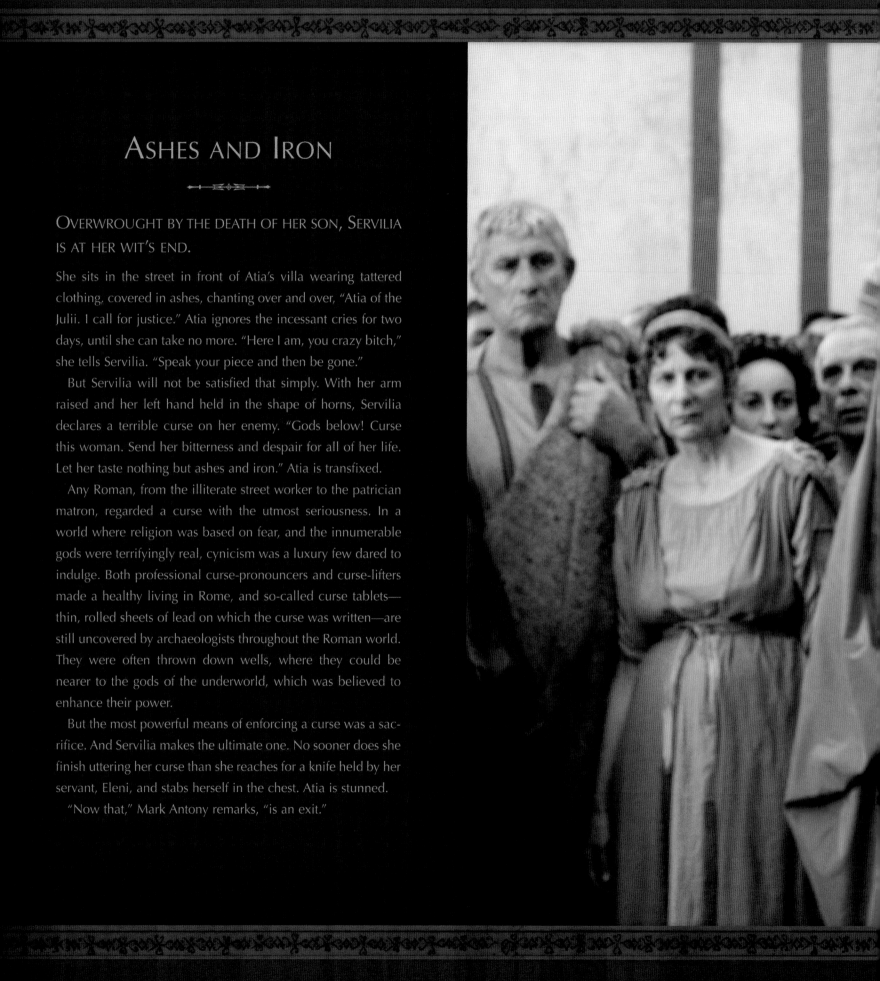

ASHES AND IRON

⊢━◈━⊣

OVERWROUGHT BY THE DEATH OF HER SON, SERVILIA
IS AT HER WIT'S END.

She sits in the street in front of Atia's villa wearing tattered
clothing, covered in ashes, chanting over and over, "Atia of the
Julii. I call for justice." Atia ignores the incessant cries for two
days, until she can take no more. "Here I am, you crazy bitch,"
she tells Servilia. "Speak your piece and then be gone."

But Servilia will not be satisfied that simply. With her arm
raised and her left hand held in the shape of horns, Servilia
declares a terrible curse on her enemy. "Gods below! Curse
this woman. Send her bitterness and despair for all of her life.
Let her taste nothing but ashes and iron." Atia is transfixed.

Any Roman, from the illiterate street worker to the patrician
matron, regarded a curse with the utmost seriousness. In a
world where religion was based on fear, and the innumerable
gods were terrifyingly real, cynicism was a luxury few dared to
indulge. Both professional curse-pronouncers and curse-lifters
made a healthy living in Rome, and so-called curse tablets—
thin, rolled sheets of lead on which the curse was written—are
still uncovered by archaeologists throughout the Roman world.
They were often thrown down wells, where they could be
nearer to the gods of the underworld, which was believed to
enhance their power.

But the most powerful means of enforcing a curse was a sacrifice. And Servilia makes the ultimate one. No sooner does she
finish uttering her curse than she reaches for a knife held by her
servant, Eleni, and stabs herself in the chest. Atia is stunned.

"Now that," Mark Antony remarks, "is an exit."

To solidify Octavian and Mark Antony's alliance, Atia proposes a marriage between the two families. To her delight, both men agree. She duly gets a wedding—but it is not her own. Octavian insists that Antony marry his sister, Octavia, Atia's daughter, instead.

DEATH COMES UNEXPECTEDLY TO THE AVENTINE. The heavily pregnant Eirene miscarries. Pullo cannot bear to face the truth, but Eirene simply asks if the lost child was a girl or a boy. A boy, Pullo replies. "Then bury him with me," she says.

Everywhere dreams are unraveling. Vorenus discovers that his elder daughter, Vorena, has betrayed him. She is sleeping with a man from a rival gang and disclosing the secrets of the Aventine Collegium. Heartbroken, he angrily confronts her, "It was you who betrayed me. . . . Why would you do that?" Vorena is enraged. "You killed my mother. You cursed me to Hades," she accuses him. "And you ask why. Because I hate you. I hate you. We all hate you." Pushed too far, Vorenus attacks her. Pullo intervenes, and Vorenus realizes his younger children are watching in terror. Vorenus has been lying to himself: he cannot create a happy family from the ashes of their former lives. He decides he must leave the Aventine.

A Virtuous Woman

Octavian has marriage in mind, and a match is made with Livia Drusilla. She is already married to another man and pregnant by him. But for Octavian, this is a mere technicality. She will simply divorce and marry him instead.

In the late Roman Republic, divorce had become common, particularly among the richest families. Marriages were regarded as unions arranged for social and economic benefit rather than romantic attachments, and divorce was seen in a similarly pragmatic light.

In terms of social and economic benefit, prospective wives did not come more beneficial than Livia. She was from the clan of the Claudii, the most noble of all Roman families. Her connections were impeccable. It was little wonder that Octavian did everything he could to secure his match with her.

Livia exercised considerable influence over Octavian, and at his death he left her one-third of his estate, making her by far the most formidable and wealthy woman in Rome.

Livia and Octavian remained married until the end of his life, in 14 A.D. By then, he had become emperor and assumed the title "Augustus." After his death, Livia continued to wield influence over his successor, her son from her previous marriage, Tiberius. In fact, her bloodline would dominate Rome for four generations. Her son Tiberius, grandson Claudius, great grandson Caligula, and great great grandson Nero would all become emperor.

Even in matters of the heart, Octavian's instinct for power is unerring.

At a family gathering, Octavian confronts Mark Antony with news that his spies have discovered. Despite being married to Octavia, Antony is sleeping with her mother, Atia. And he has learned that Octavia has been carrying on her own affair, with his right-hand man, Marcus Agrippa. Octavian wants Antony to leave the city, or he will reveal the disgrace to all of Rome. Antony threatens Octavian with violence, but Octavian is no longer a boy to be intimidated. Striking Octavian would start a civil war. Antony has no choice but to leave for Egypt.

The gang warfare that has been seething in Rome's streets finally boils over. Vorenus has followed Mark Antony to Egypt, and Pullo, now captain of the Aventine gang, seeks revenge on the gang members who have betrayed them. Pullo's overwhelming grief and rage propels him forward to victory as he hacks a bloody swath through the opposing gangs.

ANTONY AND CLEOPATRA

ALEXANDRIA PROVES A DEAD END FOR MARK ANTONY.
ISOLATED FROM ROME AND FROM POWER, HE CAN
ONLY DREAM OF THE INFLUENCE HE HAS LOST.

His life with Cleopatra in Alexandria is one of excess and
debauchery. She is a jealous lover and wields unlimited
influence over him. Bleary-eyed, drunk, and wearing traditional Egyptian court dress, he hardly resembles the successful Roman soldier he once was.

Antony does have some leverage: he controls the grain supply that feeds the city of Rome. And Octavian is becoming desperate as the city supply dwindles. He goes so far as to offer to
triple the price of the grain. Antony refuses and Cleopatra suggests they declare war on Rome. But Antony wants to return
home a savior of the people, not a conqueror.

OCTAVIAN DISPATCHES OCTAVIA AND ATIA TO ALEXANDRIA, knowing that Antony will appease Cleopatra by refusing to see his Roman wife. It is an insult that the patriotic Roman people will not forgive. Barred at the gates of Cleopatra's palace, all mother and daughter can do is to await their audience with increasing frustration. Dejected, they return to Rome. Octavian now has the reason he needs to declare war on Antony.

Gaia is mortally wounded defending Pullo in a fight. With Pullo vigilant at her deathbed,
Gaia reveals a terrible secret. "I can't go to the afterlife with lies in my heart," says Gaia.
"It was me who killed Eirene and your child. I wanted you for myself, so I poisoned her."
Without a word Pullo places his hands on Gaia's neck and strangles her. He casts her
corpse in the river—like trash.

MARK ANTONY IS DEFEATED BY OCTAVIAN IN A BATTLE FOUGHT AT ACTIUM, off the shores of Greece. Antony returns to Alexandria; Octavian follows and besieges the city. Cleopatra suggests they try to escape Alexandria, but Antony knows that death is the only option. He chooses the route of honorable suicide, with the help of Vorenus, who has remained faithful to Antony during his exile in Egypt. Vorenus asks Antony if he has any last instructions. "Just tell the people I died well. I died Roman," he says. And then Antony impales himself on a sword held by Vorenus. As a mark of respect, Vorenus dresses Antony in his full Roman regalia and seats his corpse in the throne room of the Ptolemies.

Octavian offers Cleopatra a deal: Antony's life for her safety. But when she realizes he means to parade her in chains through the streets of Rome, she too chooses death over surrender. An asp is smuggled into her chambers. Octavian walks into the throne room too late to stop her. "You have a rotten soul," she whispers in his ear as she takes her last breath.

Vorenus flees the palace with Cleopatra's son, Caesarion. He knows that Octavian, believing Caesarion to be Caesar's son and a rival to power, will kill him if he can. But Vorenus wants to unite Caesarion with his real father.

Octavian orders Pullo to find Caesarion and kill him. Pullo has different plans for his son. He finds Vorenus and Caesarion in the desert. Together they decide to ride south to safety. Pullo hopes to convince Vorenus to return to Rome, but Vorenus insists that he will only travel with them as far as Judea. Pullo is not the only Roman looking for Caesarion. When he and Vorenus come across a platoon of soldiers, they must fight to protect Caesarion's life. They are successful, but Vorenus is gravely wounded.

"I don't want to die in this fucking shithole," he tells Pullo. "I want to see my children. Take me home."

AGAINST THE ODDS, PULLO MANAGES TO BRING VORENUS BACK
TO ROME ALIVE, where he is reunited with Lyde and his children. On his
deathbed, the family makes amends and Vorenus is able to die in peace.

Octavian returns from Egypt and, just like Caesar before him, he is awarded a Triumph. He requires his family to attend, but Atia is despondent over the death of Antony. She can find no happiness in being the mother of the first citizen of Rome. But at the last minute she arrives, dazzling in her most powerful dress, and sweeps to the head of the procession. Livia icily objects. "You will find if you consult the priests the wife takes precedence," she informs Atia with a perfect hostess smile. But Atia has never been a woman to give in so easily. "I'll not let a vicious little trollop like you walk ahead of me. I go first. I know who you are. I can see you. You are swearing now that some day you will destroy me. Remember, far better women than you have sworn to do the same. Go and look for them now."

OCTAVIAN'S TRIUMPH

RIDING IN A CHARIOT DRAWN BY FOUR WHITE HORSES, OCTAVIAN BASKS IN THE ADULATION OF THE ROMAN CROWD. THE TEENAGE BOY—WHOM NONE SAW FIT TO TAKE SERIOUSLY—HAS COMPLETED AN ASTONISHING JOURNEY. HE IS WITHOUT QUESTION OR RIVAL THE MOST POWERFUL MAN IN THE WORLD.

Three years after the deaths of Mark Antony and Cleopatra, the Senate, which Octavian controls completely, voted to give Octavian a new title: Augustus, "Revered One." Octavian feigned reluctance and hesitated to accept it.

But no one was fooled. In practice he demanded reverence. And the Roman people were only too happy to oblige. After nearly a century of civil war, Augustus had brought them stability. In turn, they rewarded him with a power that was virtually without limit. He was king in all but name.

Still proud of the ideals of the Republic, the Romans stopped short of using that hateful term. So Augustus goes down in history not as a king, but as an emperor. He was the first of the Roman emperors, and the greatest. He ruled for forty-one years, longer than any of the emperors who succeeded him.

Octavian transformed the world he governed, beginning with Rome. He was determined to make Rome a worthy imperial capital. "I found her a city of brick," he wrote at the end of his life, "and left her a city of marble." But the changes he wrought were more profound than that.

Octavian consolidated the economy, reorganized the army, and reestablished order at home and abroad. More than any one man, he was responsible for creating what we call the Roman Empire, a political entity that had a more profound effect on future human history than any other. For these achievements it is not ridiculous to describe him as the most brilliant and influential politician who has ever lived. In absolute terms, he was also perhaps the most powerful.

As for the price that he paid to achieve that power? That only he can know.

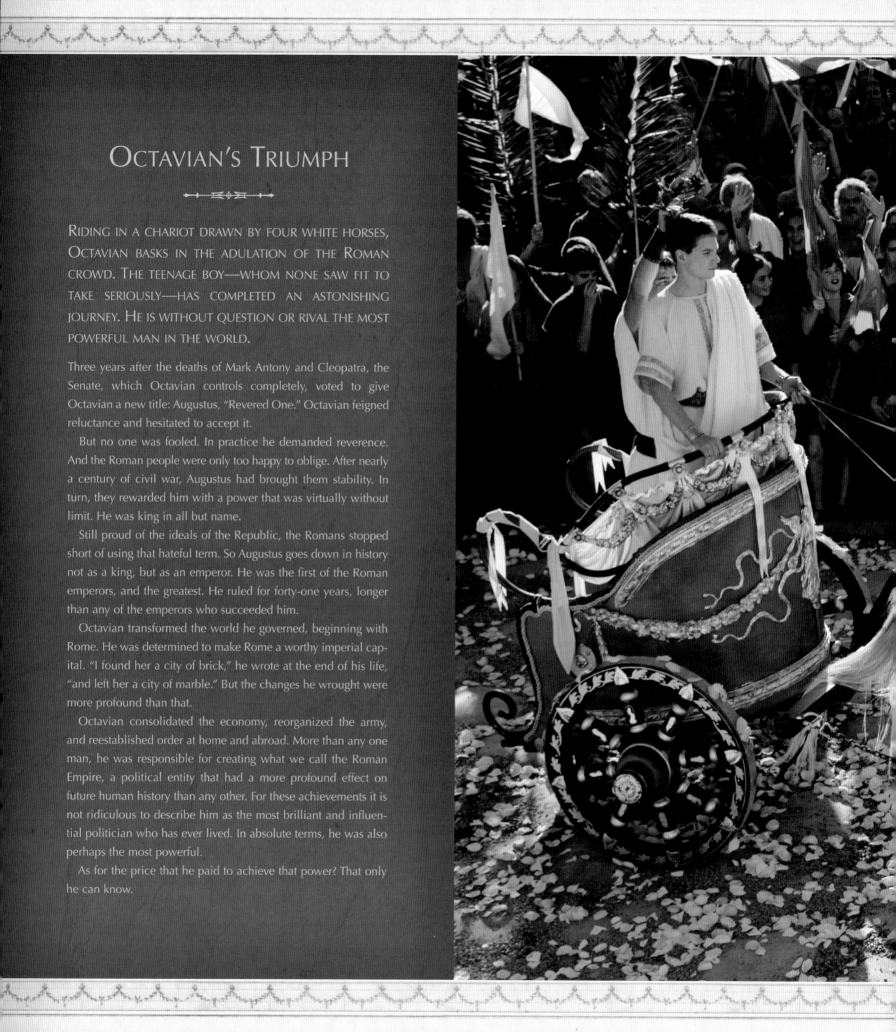

BUILDING ROME

"I ALWAYS DREAMED OF DOING A BIG BACKLOT NUMBER AT THE CINECITTÀ," SAYS *ROME* PRODUCTION DESIGNER JOSEPH BENNETT. "AND THEN HBO RANG ME UP AND ASKED ME TO DO JUST THAT."

Cinecittà Studios, just outside Rome, is the fabled location of some of the screen's greatest depictions of the classical world, including *Ben Hur* and *Cleopatra*. Indeed, the studio is synonymous with grand scale. It was the perfect place for HBO to undertake the most ambitious recreation of ancient Rome ever attempted on television.

The five-acre backlot was almost entirely turned over to the creation of *Rome*, making it one of the largest single television sets in the world. "The ethos was to create a location, rather than just a set," Bennett explains. "It was the opposite of the blue-screen digital approach, or a design that allows just a few magnificent grandstand-

ing shots, but little flexibility. It was about being real, as a contemporary drama like *The Sopranos*, shot in New Jersey, is real. A drama like that utilizes its environment. That was what HBO wanted for *Rome*. They wanted us to create a real environment."

For its massive scale and exacting attention to detail, the work was done at amazing speed. Construction began in September 2003 and the set was ready for filming by the following March. The exteriors of the buildings were constructed from fiberglass, concrete, resin, and plastic and finished to resemble wood or stone. "The standard of craftsmanship in Italy is extraordinarily high," says Bennett. "The finish was so convincing that many people could not believe that original materials had not been used. When I showed visitors the Forum, they were amazed that there was not a single piece of stone."

No sooner was the construction finished than the next stage began: making the buildings look as if they had been standing for several hundred years, rather than built the previous week. "Distressing and aging the set was part of the initial concept," explains Bennett. "Rome itself was not a new city. There was always building going on.

We took modern Rome as an inspiration, but we also looked at Third World cities, too: Calcutta, Mexico City, São Paulo. You've got to break out of the perceived image of a city of white pillars and white togas. There were a million people squeezed into a relatively small area. Rome was seething with people, alive with smoke and color, broken down, and patched up."

The vibrant colors of both the backlot and the interiors, constructed on separate sound stages, were sourced from Roman originals, recovered from well-preserved sites such as Pompeii. "The biggest single surprise for a time-traveler would have to be the color," says Bennett. "It was a riot. It would have been like walking around in Thailand, all gold and crazy, bright colors. The absolute opposite of our perceived impressions of ancient Rome, which mainly come from nineteenth-century paintings where everything is in boring white."

Authenticity was the watchword, but the set was not a facsimile of an ancient Roman original. *Rome*'s Forum was modified both for dramatic and aesthetic purposes. The Temple of Jupiter was moved from its location on the Capitoline Hill (a part of Rome that the series never constructed) into the Forum because it was a central location in several scripts. *Rome*'s Senate House was reconstructed as a round chamber, its curves making it a more rewarding space in which to film. In reality the Senate House was rectangular.

"We were asked to create a real space and that's what we did," says Bennett. "When you were physically in it, it was as if you were in Rome. Everywhere you looked, it was Rome. And it was organic; it was able to develop over time, which is a luxury you don't have on a big movie. It was a once-in-a-lifetime opportunity."

OPPOSITE: A set-dressing sketch for the opening episode of *Rome*. Set dressing, under the supervision of Cristina Onori, was an essential part of achieving the completed look. It is the art of transforming a bare structure into a real, "liveable" space, in which it's possible to imagine that the inhabitants have just put down whatever they were doing and will walk back in once the camera starts rolling.

ABOVE: This angle looks into the Forum along the *Via Sacra* or Sacred Way. The carts, stalls, awnings, and construction tower visible were all made in Italy especially for the show.

≫ THE STREETS OF ROME ≪

It was not only the monumental spaces of ancient Rome that were reconstructed for the show. More than a third of the backlot was devoted to the construction of the *Subura*, Rome's most notorious slum. This space also doubled for parts of the Aventine Hill, home to Vorenus and Niobe. These multistoried wooden buildings were known as *insulae* in Latin, which literally means "islands" but is better translated as "apartment buildings."

Every square inch of ground floor space in areas like the *Subura* was given over to shops and commercial activity. There was a wide variety of commerce in Rome, with different trades concentrated on specific streets. The Roman playwright Plautus mused on the variety of commercial activity in Rome, "There are clothes cleaners, clothes dyers, goldsmiths, wool weavers, lace-makers, lace-sellers, veil-makers, sellers of purple dye, sellers of yellow dye, makers of muffs and shoemakers who add balsam scent to their shoes, linen sellers, bootmakers, cobblers, slipper makers, sandal makers, fabric stainers, sellers of every kind of produce, those who work every kind of metal."

TEMPLE OF JUPITER

THE TEMPLE OF JUPITER IS A CENTRAL SETTING IN THE STORY OF *ROME*. ALTHOUGH ITS TRUE HISTORICAL LOCATION IS ON THE CAPITOLINE HILL, THE SET DESIGNERS RE-CREATED THE ROMAN FORUM WITH THE TEMPLE AT ITS CENTER.

The sketch details have nearly all been carefully realized in the actual construction, for example, in the Corinthian capitals of the pillars and sweeping steps.

The Temple of Jupiter was the most important of all temples in ancient Rome. Jupiter was universally acknowledged as the king of the gods and his central temple was known as *Iupiter Optimus Maximus*, which literally means "Jupiter, Best and Biggest."

Today its remains are almost completely hidden beneath the museums that have been constructed on Rome's Capitoline Hill. One small part of the temple base can be seen in the flank of the modern *Palazzo dei Conservatori*.

⇒ THE ART OF ROME ⇐

Artistically, Rome at the end of the Republic was a city in transition, as many of the architectural details from the backlot set featured here indicate.

All the motifs, from the lyre-carrying attendants of the gods on the temple pediment to the classic drinking party scene, or *symposium*, painted on a wall on the streets of Rome to the intricate stone carving depicting the mythological battle between the centaurs and their barbarian enemy, the Lapiths are of the influence of Greek art and culture.

For centuries Rome resisted the influence of Greece. When the Romans conquered Greece in a military campaign some 150 years before the birth of Christ, it was regarded as a sign of Roman superiority. But with time, Rome gradually came to admit that, in artistic terms, Greece had perfected a style that Rome could only hope to imitate and never come to surpass. *Hellenisation*, or the growing influence of Greece, was the most significant cultural development of the day.

The Roman poet Horace summed it up best when he wrote, "Greece has taken its savage captor captive."

ATIA'S VILLA

Atia's villa was one of the most elaborate sets created by *Rome*'s production team. The interiors, constructed on sound stages at Cinecittà, consisted of more than fifteen complete rooms.

Filled with many luxuries, the villa exemplified the lifestyle of a typical patrician Roman. Gianpaolo Rifino created this stunning set-dressing sketch of the homecoming party that Atia throws for Julius Caesar (top right). The sketch illustrates how set decorator Cristina Onori's initial ideas were translated into reality.

The party took place in the villa's central courtyard, the *atrium*. Pillars made of expensive stone, such as Numidian porphyry, traditionally surrounded the atrium. The small pool at the center of the atrium was called the *impluvium*.

Across the atrium are curved niches in the wall that hold a series of busts. These are portraits of the family's ancestors, specifically those who held important political posts. The busts are linked by red ribbon, which clarified the nature of the relationship—father, uncle, cousin—between the different people represented. The patrician families would have had many important ancestors.

The mosaic floor is based on a Roman original unearthed at Pompeii. It's an abstract fishing scene that shows traditional fish caught in the Bay of Naples. The fishermen are idealized in the Greek style. The Bay of Naples was the equivalent of the French Riviera; it was the single most desirable stretch of real estate in the area and a playground of the ultra-rich.

From set sketch to reality was a careful process, but the final product was a beautiful and authentic room that created the perfect backdrop for patrician intrigue.

❧ INSIDE ROME'S VILLAS ❧

Joseph Bennett and his team of set designers painstakingly crafted luxurious interiors for the show's patrician villas. The attention to detail is exquisite. The light blue walls and intricate molding in Servilia's atrium reflect her subtle and elegant style. The elaborate murals in Atia's bedroom and alcove are an indication of her wealth and status in Roman society. Mural styles were constantly changing, and it was important to keep up with the latest trends. Sophisticated observers could identify the quality of work by the colors used and the sophistication of the details and perspective. The sketch of Caesar's bedroom by Gianpaolo Rifino shows a more masculine side of the villa interiors, with bold columns and fewer decorative murals.

ROME - 12° EP - SET DRESSING - CESAR'S BEDROOM

SET DECORATOR: CRISTINA ONORI
SKETCH: GIANPAOLO RIFINO

AFTERWORD

BY JONATHAN STAMP

✦ ⋇✧⋇ ✦

You should start early to get the best light. There's also less traffic then, and you'll be going against what little there is. Cross the river into Trastevere, swing onto Via Garibaldi, and you'll start to climb. The road winds up past the beautiful, intimate Church of San Pietro in Montorio. At a fork by the Botanical Gardens, you turn right. You can park in a little square directly beneath the imposing statue of Garibaldi. And then it's just a few steps from your car. Walk up to the low wall, and look.

There it is, the view from the hill the Italians call the Gianicolo, the most beautiful view of the most beautiful city in the world. Rome, the Eternal City.

It's rightly said that you could live in Rome all your life and never know her secrets. But from the Gianicolo, it feels as though you can take it all in at a glance. From the Bronze Age huts on the wooded hill of the Palatine, to the majesty of St. Peter's Cathedral, to the chill marble of the Vittorio Emmanuele II memorial, it is as if every generation has left its monument. Nowhere else on earth is human history so densely and chaotically packed. This is one sense in which Rome is the Eternal City. But there is a deeper sense in which it deserves to be called so. For Rome has become more than the material reality spread before you on the Gianicolo. Rome has become a myth.

It is a myth because Rome's story is one to which every subsequent age has turned to understand and make sense of itself. It is a familiar, resonant, and significant story. Every generation that has held up the mirror of the Roman myth has seen something different reflected there, but for each it has served its purpose.

Rome's mythical power derives not just from its familiarity but its flexibility. It encompasses the extremes of human experience, from duty, fortitude, and self-denial to absolutism, corruption, and obscene excess. It is as a myth that Rome is truly eternal, and that is the sense in which it will remain so.

Rome captures our generation's reflection of itself. But there were visions of Rome before, and there will be new visions to come. The poet Byron wrote:

> *While stands the Coliseum, Rome shall stand;*
> *When falls the Coliseum, Rome will fall;*
> *And when Rome falls—the world.*

EPISODE GUIDE
≈ SEASON ONE ≈

EPISODE I
THE STOLEN EAGLES

WRITTEN BY BRUNO HELLER, DIRECTED BY MICHAEL APTED

A power struggle is brewing in Rome. After an eight-year campaign, Gaius Julius Caesar achieves victory in Gaul. His son-in-law, friend, and co-consul of the Republic, Pompey Magnus, is pressured by elder Senate members to renounce the popular Caesar, whose homecoming, they worry, will disrupt the balance of power. When Pompey's wife, Caesar's daughter, dies in childbirth, Caesar's calculating niece, Atia, offers her own daughter, Octavia, to be Pompey's new bride. She also dispatches her young son, Octavian, on a dangerous journey to Gaul to deliver a prized steed to Caesar. When Caesar's gold standard, the very symbol of his power, is stolen, an unlikely partnership is born. Two members of the famed Thirteenth Legion, the honorable Centurion Lucius Vorenus and rebellious Legionnaire Titus Pullo, are recruited to retrieve it. They accomplish their mission threefold, rescuing the captured Octavian, recovering Caesar's standard, and taking the head of the man who stole it—Pompey's chief attendant.

EPISODE IV
STEALING FROM SATURN

WRITTEN BY BRUNO HELLER, DIRECTED BY JULIAN FARINO

Having left Rome, Pompey insists his faction is maneuvering, not fleeing. When he learns Caesar does not have the Treasury, he is heartened, predicting that the people of Rome will rebel against Caesar. In Rome, Caesar declares martial law. Mark Antony asks Vorenus to rejoin the army for a handsome price, but he declines. Seeking the good will of local merchants for their new business, Vorenus and Niobe hold a dinner. Niobe's distraught sister, Lyde, nearly reveals the true identity of infant Lucius's father and breaks the statue of Janus, a bad omen. Atia hosts a dinner honoring Caesar. Octavian witnesses Caesar's debilitating affliction—a grand mal seizure. Servilia is passionately reunited with Caesar. Pompey's son Quintus visits Vorenus and demands the Treasury, only to be interrupted by Pullo. Vorenus convinces Pullo to return the gold (and Quintus) to Caesar. Caesar sends an offer of truce to Pompey via his son, but his rival rejects the terms.

EPISODE V
THE RAM HAS TOUCHED THE WALL

WRITTEN BY BRUNO HELLER, DIRECTED BY ALLEN COULTER

Pompey agrees to a cessation of hostilities with Caesar, asserting that it's not a surrender. Caesar decides to pursue Pompey, and to avoid public criticism, ascribes his aggressiveness to his enemy's unwillingness to meet face to face. Atia publicly exposes Caesar's affair with Servilia. When Caesar's wife threatens divorce, he is forced to end the relationship. Atia hires Pullo to teach Octavian how to be a man. Octavian and Pullo kill Lyde's husband, Evander, after they coerce him to reveal the truth about his relationship with Niobe and the baby Lucius. The two decide Vorenus must never know that Evander is the father. Vorenus's slave business falters and he is forced to take a job with a debt collector. When he is asked to kill a man, he quits and accepts Mark Antony's offer to return to the army. Servilia curses Atia for her treachery. Caesar finally reaches the coast, but Pompey has already sailed for Greece.

EPISODE II

HOW TITUS PULLO BROUGHT DOWN THE REPUBLIC

WRITTEN BY BRUNO HELLER, DIRECTED BY MICHAEL APTED

Caesar appoints Mark Antony the People's Tribune, sending him to Rome to negotiate with Pompey. Pullo and Vorenus return to Rome. Vorenus arrives home after eight years to find his wife, Niobe, holding an infant—who he learns is his grandchild. Pullo heads for the taverns and kills a man after a night of gambling in Pompey-friendly territory turns sour. Antony meets with Pompey and the senators. The proposal—giving Caesar control of a province and legal immunity—offends Pompey, as was intended. Pompey forces Cicero to support a Senate ultimatum to put Caesar on trial. When the vote is called, chaos erupts, and Antony's veto goes unheard. A technicality allows him to oppose the motion the next day, but when Pompey loyalists attack Pullo in the Forum—payback for the earlier murder—Antony thinks he is being attacked. Caesar is moved to declare war, and sets out with his army for Rome.

EPISODE III

AN OWL IN A THORNBUSH

WRITTEN BY BRUNO HELLER, DIRECTED BY MICHAEL APTED

Caesar dispatches a scout party led by Vorenus and Pullo to size up Pompey's defenses. Pompey is shocked to learn Caesar's men are just thirty miles outside the city and decides that a tactical retreat is necessary. He instructs his top aide to secure the Treasury, which is swiftly stolen by the underling Appius. With an angry mob gathering outside Atia's villa, Octavia sneaks out to spend one last night with her husband. Angered, Atia retaliates by having him killed. Brutus sides with Pompey, while his mother, Servilia, remains in Rome awaiting the return of her lover, Caesar. Niobe's brother-in-law visits her and demands to see his son, the infant Lucius. Vorenus and Pullo encounter Appius leaving town and a battle ensues; Appius escapes, but without the wagon of gold. The duo make their way into a deserted Rome. Vorenus posts Caesar's peaceful proclamation in the Forum, promptly quits the army, and heads home to make amends with Niobe. Pullo returns to the abandoned wagon and discovers the missing gold.

EPISODE VI

EGERIA

WRITTEN BY JOHN MILIUS AND BRUNO HELLER, DIRECTED BY ALAN POUL

With Caesar off at war, Mark Antony pushes laws through the Senate making Caesar co-consul. At Atia's request, Pullo takes Octavian to a high-end brothel to lose his virginity. Pullo tells Niobe and Lyde that Evander was killed over gambling debts. The sisters fight, and Niobe insists Evander instigated their affair. Caesar finds himself greatly outnumbered in Greece and summons his Thirteenth Legion from Rome. Antony rejects an opportunity to betray Caesar, as well as Atia's proposal to form an alliance against her uncle through marriage. Atia tries to curry Servilia's good will by giving her a well-endowed slave and a bejeweled tortoise. She sends Octavian to an academy out of harm's way. Antony, Vorenus, Pullo, and the Thirteenth Legion encounter deadly seas on the way to Greece.

EPISODE VII

PHARSALUS

WRITTEN BY DAVID FRANKEL, DIRECTED BY TIM VAN PATTEN

Pompey wants to let Caesar's army wither. But the senators insist he must make a decisive attack to assert his power and restore honor to the Republic; he acquiesces. News of Caesar's fate reaches Rome, and Atia sends Octavia to Servilia to ask for protection. Lyde and Niobe make amends. Vorenus and Pullo wash ashore on a deserted island after the Thirteenth Legion is shipwrecked. They cheat death by fashioning a raft using the corpses of their comrades. Despite his depleted army, Caesar defeats Pompey. Cato and Scipio part ways with Pompey when he decides to flee to Egypt, while Brutus and Cicero surrender to a merciful Caesar. Vorenus and Pullo land in Greece and come face to face with Pompey. Vorenus decides to spare Pompey and later informs an irate Caesar of his decision. Caesar follows Pompey to Egypt, but the defeated leader is murdered as he sets foot on Egyptian soil.

EPISODE VIII
CAESARION

WRITTEN BY WILLIAM J. MACDONALD, DIRECTED BY STEPHEN SHILL

Caesar arrives in Egypt and meets the child king Ptolemy XIII, whose throne is challenged by his sister, Cleopatra. When Ptolemy presents Pompey's head to him, Caesar angrily demands the surrender of the man who murdered his rival. He sends Mark Antony back to Rome with half the legion, and remains in Egypt to prevent civil war and preserve Rome's grain supply. He appoints himself adjudicator of the struggle for the Egyptian throne. Vorenus and Pullo rescue the imprisoned Cleopatra from Ptolemy's assassins. When Cleopatra informs her slave that she is ripe to conceive, Vorenus is instructed to have sex with her; he refuses, but Pullo happily complies. Ptolemy and his advisors are killed. Cleopatra and Caesar unite in politics and sex in Alexanderia as a battle rages outside. In Rome, Brutus and Cicero contemplate an alliance with Cato and Scipio, only to be overheard and rebuked by Antony. In Egypt, Caesar and Cleopatra present their newborn son to their followers.

EPISODE IX
UTICA

WRITTEN BY ALEXANDRA CUNNINGHAM, DIRECTED BY JEREMY PODESWA

Cato and Scipio commit suicide following a final defeat against Caesar. Caesar and his men return to Rome victorious. Vorenus finds Niobe running a successful butcher shop, while Pullo seeks out Eirene. Vorenus interferes with a street quarrel and offends a powerful merchant, who threatens to harm Vorenus's wife and children if he does not receive a public apology. With thugs gathering outside Vorenus's villa, Caesar appears to offer him a magistrate position, which he reluctantly accepts. Bent on destroying Caesar, Servilia wants to uncover the leader's affliction. She manipulates her lover, Octavia, by revealing that it was Atia who killed Octavia's husband. In hopes of discovering the secret, Octavia seduces Octavian, only to be condemned by her brother for her trickery. Word of their union reaches Atia, who adamantly denies Servilia's claims. Servilia does not learn of Caesar's affliction, but she does learn another dangerous secret. Atia exacts revenge by having Servilia attacked on the streets.

EPISODE XII
KALENDS OF FEBRUARY

WRITTEN BY BRUNO HELLER, DIRECTED BY ALAN TAYLOR

Pullo and Vorenus are heroes after their gladiatorial triumph. Vorenus welcomes home a still infirm Pullo, but Eirene tries to kill him. Caesar creates a hundred new senator positions, angering the Republic's old guard; they are even more astonished when he makes Vorenus a senator. His new appointee is always at his side. The Servilia-led faction bemoans the protection Vorenus offers Caesar and debates murdering him at his most vulnerable. Brutus insists that Caesar be executed on the Senate floor, in daylight. As Caesar and Vorenus approach the Senate, Servilia's servant informs Vorenus of the true patronage of infant Lucius and he rushes home, leaving Caesar unprotected. When confronted, Niobe commits suicide. In the Senate, Casca strikes the first blow, and chaos ensues as the conspirators rush forward, stabbing wildly. Caesar falls to the ground, and Cassius orders Brutus to make his move. Brutus mortally stabs Caesar. In the countryside, Pullo walks with Eirene, unaware of the trouble in Rome.

≈ SEASON TWO ≈

EPISODE X
TRIUMPH

WRITTEN BY ADRIAN HODGES, DIRECTED BY ALAN TAYLOR

In a public display of loyalty, Cicero and Brutus move the Senate to name Caesar emperor, and the ruling is carried unanimously. Caesar warns Brutus he will not forgive the young man twice. Atia visits a beleaguered Servilia to invite her to Caesar's Triumph, an offer Servilia refuses. Octavia flees to the Temple of Cybele, where she hopes to cleanse herself of weakness. Octavian arrives to retrieve her, saying her absence at Caesar's ceremony will reflect badly on the family. To prepare for the Triumph, Octavian anoints Caesar with ox's blood. The King of Gaul is publicly executed during the Triumph. Vorenus begins his campaign for magistrate, only to learn the election is rigged to ensure his victory. Servilia welcomes Pompey's vengeful son, Quintus, into her home, and together they begin an underground campaign against Caesar, using Brutus's name. With the hope of marrying Eirene, Pullo enlists Vorenus's help and money to free her. But he enrages Vorenus when he kills Eirene's lover. Vorenus tries to fight Pullo, and the two part bitterly.

EPISODE XI
THE SPOILS

WRITTEN BY BRUNO HELLER, DIRECTED BY MIKAEL SALOMON

Out of options, Pullo takes a job as a petty hit man; when he kills a critic of Caesar's, he is imprisoned and charged with murder. Magistrate Vorenus is hearing citizens' complaints, including those of former fellow soldier Mascius and his comrades, who want land in Italy. Caesar proposes offering them land in undesirable Polonia, as well as a personal bribe to sway Mascius. Mascius accepts. Graffiti depicting Brutus stabbing Caesar in the back appears all over town. Despite Brutus's steadfast loyalty to Caesar, both Servilia and Cassius insist that, due to his lineage, Brutus must be the one to kill his friend. Atia warns Caesar of Brutus's betrayal. Facing death in the arena, Pullo refuses to fight, but when gladiators insult the Thirteenth Legion he erupts in fury, killing them all and defiantly crying, "Thirteen!" Finally weakened by yet another onslaught, Pullo is saved by Vorenus. Caesar informs Brutus he wishes him to leave Rome and rule Macedonia; Brutus declines and, ultimately, switches allegiances.

EPISODE XIII
PASSOVER

WRITTEN BY BRUNO HELLER, DIRECTED BY TIM VAN PATTEN

Caesar lies dead on the Senate floor. Mark Antony rushes to Atia, and they prepare to flee to the north. While in the country, Pullo proposes to Eirene. Caesar's will is read and it names Octavian his son and sole heir. Octavian insists he remain in the city, pointing out Brutus and Cassius's legal bind: if Caesar is declared a tyrant, all positions are null and void; if he is not, the law, which would rule them murderers, will stand. Antony presents this logic to Brutus and Servilia, and proposes amnesty for them and a public funeral for Caesar. Brutus accepts. Antony kills Quintus. Vorenus's children return home to find their father cradling the dead body of their mother. Grief-stricken, Vorenus curses his children. Antony's passionate speech at the public funeral creates an angry mob. When Vorenus returns from Niobe's funeral pyre, he learns that Erastes's men have killed his children and sister-in-law, Lyde; he and Pullo seek revenge and murder Erastes. Brutus escapes the city with Cassius.

EPISODE XIV
SON OF HADES

WRITTEN BY BRUNO HELLER, DIRECTED BY ALLEN COULTER

With Erastes dead, gang war rages in the streets. Vorenus is despondent. Mark Antony is dismissive of Octavian's requests for his money and is pressed by Cicero to quell the violence in the Aventine. Cleopatra comes to Rome and demands her son Caesarion be publicly declared Caesar's son; Antony refuses. Pullo enlists Antony's help to rally Vorenus. Antony offers Vorenus the chance to redeem himself by restoring order to the Aventine. Vorenus accepts the charge, and at a peaceful summit of rival gangs he claims ownership of the Aventine, declaring that anyone who opposes him is his enemy. When met with resistance, he smashes a sacred statue shouting, "I am a Son of Hades!" and silencing his detractors. Octavian borrows money against his position as Caesar to pay the public. As a result, he and Antony fight bitterly. Servilia is delighted by the political division and suggests Brutus return, a notion Cicero condemns. Octavian leaves for his friend Marcus Agrippa's Campania.

EPISODE XV
THESE BEING THE WORDS OF
MARCUS TILLIUS CICERO

WRITTEN BY SCOTT BUCK, DIRECTED BY ALAN POUL

Vorenus's decisions cause a gang war in the Aventine and tension grows between him and Pullo, leading Pullo to reveal that he killed Evander. Forced by Vorenus, Pullo lies, saying he slept with Niobe. The two fight and Pullo leaves Rome with Eirene. Mark Antony threatens Cicero's life, demanding Cicero sway the Senate to approve his governing of Gaul. Despite Timon's protests, Levi becomes more political. Servilia plots to poison Atia. Cassius and Brutus unsuccessfully court military support in Turkey. Octavian's friend Agrippa arrives at Atia's villa and is entranced by Octavia. Cicero goes south to enlist Octavian's support. Cicero humiliates Antony in the senate; Antony leaves Rome to raise an army. Pullo finally returns to Rome, but learns Vorenus has gone with Antony. Lyde escapes and finds Pullo, telling him that Vorenus's children are alive. Pullo sets out to find Vorenus.

EPISODE XVI
TESTUDO ET LEPUS
(THE TORTOISE AND THE HARE)

WRITTEN BY TODD ELLIS KESSLER, DIRECTED BY ADAM DAVIDSON

The plot to poison Atia ends with her servant dying instead. Timon tortures a slave boy and confirms that Servilia was behind the plot. In retaliation, Servilia is kidnapped by Atia's men and tortured by Timon, but she is steadfast, and Timon sets her free when Atia insists he continue. In Turkey, Cassius and Brutus receive military support in their fight against Mark Antony. Octavian is victorious over Antony. Pullo locates Vorenus in the camp of battle-worn Antony. Octavian promises his army riches in Rome and prepares to return. He dispatches Agrippa, who informs Atia of her son's victory, and Octavia of his own affections for her. Agrippa visits Cicero, who is joyous at Octavian's victory but critical of his youthful ambition. Vorenus and Pullo find the traumatized children in a slave camp; Vorenus slits the camp's procurator's throat.

EPISODE XIX
DEATH MASK

WRITTEN BY SCOTT BUCK, DIRECTED BY JOHN MAYBURY

Devastated by Brutus's death, Servilia appears outside Atia's villa chanting, "Atia of the Julii, I call for justice." Octavian, Mark Antony, and Lepidus agree to divide rule over the empire and equitably split all revenue. When Gaia is disrespectful to Eirene, Pullo is sent to punish her, but the two end up having sex. Nearly driven mad by Servilia's chant, Atia finally faces her enemy and is met by a parting curse from Servilia, who then kills herself. Herod offers a gift to Antony to ensure his throne; when the news of the payment reaches Octavian, the rivals clash again. Memmio interrupts Vorena the Elder and Omnipor mid-tryst, and Vorena agrees to spy on her father to avoid discovery. Octavia and Agrippa's affair continues. Timon and Levi plot to kill Herod. Levi is accidentally killed when Timon decides not to go through with the assassination. Octavia and Antony are wed in a political show of unity at the behest of Octavian. Gaia visits a chemist to obtain special herbs to end a pregnancy.

EPISODE XX
A NECESSARY FICTION

WRITTEN BY TODD ELLIS KESSLER, DIRECTED BY CARL FRANKLIN

Pullo is hired to ensure the delivery of Herod's bribe, which Posca and Maecenas plot to steal. Gaia poisons Eirene, causing her to miscarry and die. Pullo is devastated, and Mascius takes his place on the job. The wagon carrying the bribe is ambushed, and only Mascius and one other survive. Convinced Posca and Mark Antony double-crossed him, Maecenas informs Octavian of the secret affairs between Antony and Atia, Agrippa and Octavia. Octavian banishes Antony to Egypt and puts Atia and Octavia under house arrest. He retains Agrippa, who severs ties with Octavia; she reveals that she's pregnant. Timon and his family leave for Jerusalem. Octavian marries Livia. Seeking the missing gold, Vorenus visits Memmio, who denies any responsibility. Mascius's interrogation ends with Vorenus discovering his daughter's betrayal, and in a fit of rage he nearly kills her. Vorenus decides to leave the city and accompanies Antony to Egypt. Pullo takes over the Aventine and delivers a brutal revenge to Memmio.

EPISODE XVII
HEROES OF THE REPUBLIC

WRITTEN BY MERE SMITH, DIRECTED BY ALIK SAKHAROV

Vorenus and Pullo return to the Aventine with the children, and Vorenus negotiates a gang truce. Octavian meets with Cicero and requests a Triumph; Cicero rejects the idea. But Cicero reluctantly agrees to make Octavian consul. Octavia visits Octavian and urges him to forgive their mother; he reminds his sister of Atia's allegiance to Mark Antony. Vorenus's children find Lyde, who advises them to feign affection for Vorenus in the name of survival. Atia successfully asks for Octavian's forgiveness. Agrippa retrieves Octavia from an orgy and declares his devotion. In the Senate, Cicero prepares to swear in Rome's youngest consul, when Octavian, supported by a phalanx of soldiers, moves to declare Brutus and Cassius enemies of the state. Cicero aligns with Brutus and Cassius, and informs Octavian that he is outnumbered. Atia comes to the rescue, going to Antony's camp and encouraging former adversaries to join forces.

EPISODE XVIII
PHILIPPI

WRITTEN BY EOGHAN MAHONY, DIRECTED BY ROBERT YOUNG

Brutus and Cassius now lead a force 100,000 strong. Octavian orders the assassination of his rivals' wealthy supporters in Rome to prevent news of his alliance with Mark Antony from leaking. The list of victims is delivered to Vorenus, who divides the killings among the gangs, and proposes using the financial gains to buy citizens fish and bread, and win their good will. After some resistance from the captains, the idea is accepted. Timon and Levi incite division among the Jews. When news of Antony and Octavian's army reaches Cicero, he hastily writes a letter warning Brutus and Cassius before Pullo arrives and kills him; the message is never delivered. Octavia and Agrippa steal a few hours of passion, even though Agrippa knows the two can never wed, an idea that Atia confirms. Eirene reveals she is pregnant. Brutus and Cassius learn they are outnumbered but choose to fight anyway. They both die in battle.

EPISODE XXI
DEUS IMPEDITIO ESURITORI NULLUS
(NO GOD CAN STOP A HUNGRY MAN)

WRITTEN BY MERE SMITH, DIRECTED BY STEPHEN SHILL

Grain supplies are dangerously low and Octavian sends a senator to Egypt to negotiate with Mark Antony, who makes outrageous demands hoping that Octavian will declare war. As the captain of the Combined Collegia, Pullo manages the city's grain supply; he keeps a caged Memmio nearby to quash deceit. Pullo goes to Octavian for help, admitting that the plebes fault him, not Antony, for the grain shortage. Octavian sends Octavia and Atia to Egypt, expecting Antony will reject his wife and anger the public. When they arrive Antony recognizes Octavian's strategy, but Cleopatra insists the women be turned away. Posca and Jocasta escape to Rome and bring with them Antony's will, which reveals his disownment of the empire. With public support, Octavian declares war. Memmio escapes and tries to kill Pullo. Gaia kills Memmio, but she is seriously wounded. On her deathbed, she tells Pullo that she poisoned Eirene. He strangles her and dumps her body in the river.

EPISODE XXII
DE PATRE VOSTRO
(ABOUT YOUR FATHER)

WRITTEN BY BRUNO HELLER, DIRECTED BY ALLAN COULTER

Mark Antony is defeated. Octavian lays siege on the palace. Vorenus remains loyal to Antony despite promises of amnesty from Octavian. Octavian offers Cleopatra a chance to save herself if she forsakes Antony. Antony decides suicide is the only option; Cleopatra agrees. When he is told that Cleopatra has killed herself, he ends his life. A deceitful and still living Cleopatra appears and sends Ceasarion away with Vorenus. When Cleopatra realizes Octavian's real intention is to take her back to Rome, she kills herself. Octavian sends Pullo in search of Vorenus and Ceasarion. He finds them in the desert. Soldiers discover the three fleeing Egypt and a battle ensues. Vorenus is badly wounded. A dying Vorenus makes peace with his children. Moments before the Triumph, Atia appears, warning Livia she cannot be defeated. Pullo tells Octavian that he killed Ceasarion. He leaves to meet Caesarion and to tell him about his father.

ACKNOWLEDGMENTS

HBO AND MELCHER MEDIA would like to thank Stacey Abiraj, Chris Albrecht, Gina Balian, Joseph Bennett, Tom Bozzelli, Barbara Compagnoni, James Costos, Daniel del Valle, Susan Ennis, April Ferry, Cara Grabowski, Bruno Heller, Courtney F. Monroe, Gurmeet Kaur, Eric Kessler, Nancy King, Jamaal Lesane, Courteney F. Monroe, Andrea Nakayama, Lauren Nathan, Martha O'Connor, Alessandra Rafferty, Lia Ronnen, Holly Rothman, Jonathan Stamp, Carolyn Strauss, Alex Tart, Shoshana Thaler, Marti Trgovich, Betty Wong, and Megan Worman. Additional thanks to all the actors, writers, directors, and crew of *Rome*.

STEPHEN SCHMIDT / DUPLEX would like to thank Gui Zong

CREDITS

All photographs are by FRANCO BICIOCCHI except as noted. All photographs © HBO, except otherwise noted.

Endpapers art © Bettmann/CORBIS. Costume sketches on pages 68, 71, 73, 75 by Robert Fletcher, courtesy of April Ferry. Set sketches on pages 124, 126, 132, 134 by Giampaolo Rifino. Architectural sketch on pages 128-129 by Egidio Spugnini. Sketch on page 136 by D. Sica. Excerpt from the Lord Byron poem *Childe Harold's Pilgrimage* appears on page 137. Quotation from Julius Caesar on page 25 is from *The Civil War* by Julius Caesar. Translation by Jonathan Stamp. Quotation from Julius Caesar on page 41 is from *Life of Caesar* by Plutarch. Translation by Jonathan Stamp. Quotations from Plutarch on page 65 are from *Life of Caesar* by Plutarch. Translation by Jonathan Stamp. Quotation from Caesar Augustus on page 122 is from *My Life* by

ROMANI IMPERII IM...

Hibernia

BRITANNIA

Londinium

ATIANTI

CVS OCE

ANVS

Celtica

Belgium

Rhenus flu.

Lutetia

GERMANIA

GALLIA

Aquitania

Helvetii

Danubius flumine

Noricum

Cantabri

Lusitania

HISPA

Pyrenei M.

Narbonensis

Rhodanus

Alpes Montes

Istria

Illyricum

Tarraco

NIA nensis

Liguria

Turci

ITAL

Flaminia

Betica

Fretum Gaditanum.

Corsica

Roma

Mare

Magn.

Ebusus Palma

Sardinia

Inferum

MARE ME

MAVRITANIA

TINGITANA

Bochi Reg.

Numidia

Sicilia

MAVRITANIA

CAESARIENSIS

AFRICA MINOR

DITERRA

Atlas mons

VRBIS AETERNAE CONDI...